POVERTY IS NOT AN OPTION

"Breaking the Chains of Financial Struggle & Walking in God's Financial Freedom"

TIMOTHY ATUNNISE

Glovim Publishing House
Atlanta, Georgia

POVERTY IS NOT AN OPTION

Copyright © 2024 by Timothy Atunnise

All rights reserved. No part of this book may be reproduced, copied, stored or transmitted in any form or by any means – graphic, electronic, or mechanical, including photocopying, recording, or information storage and retrieval systems without the prior written permission of Glovim Publishing house except where permitted by law.

Glovim Publishing House
1078 Citizens Pkwy
Suite A
Morrow, Georgia 30260

glovimbooks@gmail.com
www.glovimonline.org

Printed in the United States of America

Table of Contents

Introduction 7

The divine promise of provision 10

Breaking the chains of poverty mindset 28

Stewardship: Managing God's resources 47

The power of work and diligence 68

Overcoming financial obstacles with faith 88

Divine strategies for financial increase 108

Living a life of generosity and impact 127

Other bestselling books from the author 146

Introduction

In a world where economic hardship seems to pervade every corner, the message of hope and provision found in the Bible stands as a beacon of light. The notion that poverty is an inescapable fate is not only misleading but also contrary to the promises laid out in the Word of God. As Christians, we are called to live in the fullness of God's blessings, which includes financial freedom. This book, "Poverty Is Not An Option: Breaking the Chains of Financial Struggle & Walking in God's Financial Freedom," is a clarion call to believers to rise above the constraints of financial lack and embrace the abundant life that God has promised.

From the very beginning, God's design for humanity was one of provision and prosperity. In the Garden of Eden, Adam and Eve were placed in a setting of abundance, where every need was met without toil or struggle. This original intent reflects God's heart for His creation—He desires to bless us and see us thrive. However, the fall of man introduced sin, which brought with it not only spiritual separation from God but also physical and economic challenges. Despite this, God's plan for redemption through Jesus Christ restored not only our relationship with Him but also the promise of provision.

Throughout the Bible, we see numerous examples of God's provision. From the manna that fell from heaven to feed the Israelites in the desert, to the multiplication of loaves and fishes by Jesus to feed thousands, God's ability to provide for His people is unquestionable. These stories are not just historical accounts but are meant to inspire faith in us today. God's nature has not changed, and His promises are as relevant now as they were then.

The key to breaking free from financial struggle lies in understanding and applying the principles of God's Word. One of the fundamental truths is that God is our source. When we shift our reliance from our own abilities and circumstances to His unfailing provision, we begin to experience His supernatural supply. This does not mean we sit idly by, waiting for blessings to fall into our laps. Rather, it involves active faith—partnering with God through diligent work, wise stewardship, and generous giving.

A significant aspect of walking in financial freedom is overcoming the poverty mindset. This mindset, often rooted in fear and scarcity, can be a significant barrier to experiencing God's abundance. Renewing our minds with the truth of Scripture is essential. We must replace thoughts of lack and limitation with God's promises of provision and prosperity. This transformation begins with recognizing that our worth and success are not measured by material possessions but by our identity in Christ and our trust in His provision.

Another vital principle is stewardship. The Bible teaches us that we are managers of the resources God has entrusted to us. This includes not only our finances but also our time, talents, and opportunities. Proper stewardship involves wise management, investment, and generosity. When we honor God with our resources, we position ourselves to receive His blessings.

Work and diligence are also emphasized in Scripture as keys to financial stability. Proverbs is replete with wisdom on the benefits of hard work and the pitfalls of laziness. As we commit our work to the Lord and pursue excellence, we open the door for His favor and increase in our lives.

Ultimately, living in God's financial freedom means living a life of generosity. As we give, we reflect God's heart and activate the principle of sowing and reaping. Generosity not only meets the needs of others but also brings joy and fulfillment to the giver.

"Poverty Is Not An Option: Breaking the Chains of Financial Struggle & Walking in God's Financial Freedom" is more than a guide to financial success; it is a journey of faith. As you read through these pages, may you be inspired, challenged, and equipped to step into the abundant life that God has for you. Let us break the chains of financial struggle and walk boldly in the financial freedom that is our inheritance in Christ.

Chapter 1

The Divine Promise of Provision

Understanding God's Promise of Abundance

From the very beginning of creation, God established His desire for His children to live in abundance. The Bible is replete with promises of provision, emphasizing that poverty is not part of God's plan for His people. To understand God's promise of abundance, we must delve into the Scriptures, uncovering His heart for our well-being and His provision for our needs.

The Garden of Eden: A Model of Abundance

In Genesis 1:28-29, God blessed Adam and Eve, saying, "Be fruitful and increase in number; fill the earth and subdue it. Rule over the fish in the sea and the birds in the sky and over every living creature that moves on the ground." He provided them with everything they needed to thrive, placing them in the Garden of Eden, a place of perfect provision and abundance. This initial act of provision demonstrates God's intention for humanity to live in a state of sufficiency and prosperity.

Covenant Promises: Abraham and Beyond

God's covenant with Abraham further illustrates His promise of abundance. In Genesis 12:2-3, God tells Abraham, "I will make you into a great nation, and I will bless you; I will make your name great, and you will be a blessing. I will bless those who bless you, and whoever curses you I will curse; and all peoples on earth will be blessed through you." This covenant established not only a promise of personal blessing but also a mandate to be a channel of blessing to others.

Throughout the Old Testament, God's promises of provision continue to unfold. In Deuteronomy 28, God outlines the blessings of obedience, including prosperity in the land, fruitful harvests, and financial abundance. Verse 11 declares, "The Lord will grant you abundant prosperity—in the fruit of your womb, the young of your livestock and the crops of your ground—in the land he swore to your ancestors to give you." These promises reaffirm that God's heart is to bless His people abundantly.

Jesus: The Fulfillment of God's Promise

The New Testament brings the fulfillment of these promises through Jesus Christ. In John 10:10, Jesus declares, "The thief comes only to steal and kill and destroy; I have come that they may have life and have it to the full." Jesus came to restore what was lost through sin, including the promise of abundant life. His ministry was marked by miraculous provision, from feeding the five thousand with five loaves and two fish

(Matthew 14:13-21) to instructing Peter to find a coin in the mouth of a fish to pay the temple tax (Matthew 17:24-27).

Furthermore, Jesus teaches about God's provision in the Sermon on the Mount. In Matthew 6:25-33, He encourages His followers not to worry about their needs, emphasizing that God, who provides for the birds of the air and the flowers of the field, will certainly provide for His children. Verse 33 encapsulates this promise: "But seek first his kingdom and his righteousness, and all these things will be given to you as well." Jesus assures us that when we prioritize God's kingdom, our needs will be met abundantly.

Faith and Obedience: Keys to Unlocking Abundance

Understanding God's promise of abundance also involves recognizing the role of faith and obedience. Hebrews 11:6 states, "And without faith, it is impossible to please God, because anyone who comes to him must believe that he exists and that he rewards those who earnestly seek him." Faith is the conduit through which we receive God's promises. By trusting in His provision and aligning our lives with His will, we position ourselves to receive His blessings.

Obedience is equally crucial. Deuteronomy 28:1-2 says, "If you fully obey the Lord your God and carefully follow all his commands I give you today, the Lord your God will set you high above all the nations on earth. All these blessings will come on you and accompany you if you obey the Lord your God." Obedience to God's Word and His principles opens the door to His abundant blessings.

Embracing God's Abundance

God's promise of abundance is clear throughout Scripture. From the Garden of Eden to the teachings of Jesus, we see a consistent theme of divine provision and prosperity. As believers, we are called to embrace this promise, living in faith and obedience, and trusting that God's desire is for us to thrive and be a blessing to others. By understanding and claiming these promises, we can confidently declare that poverty is not an option for those who walk in God's provision.

Biblical Examples of Divine Provision

The Bible is replete with stories that vividly illustrate God's unwavering commitment to providing for His people. These narratives not only serve as historical accounts but also as faith-building testimonies that God's provision is not just a possibility, but a divine promise. Here, we will dig into some of the most compelling examples of divine provision, exploring their significance and the lessons they hold for believers today.

1. The Provision in the Wilderness

One of the most striking examples of God's provision is found in the story of the Israelites' journey through the wilderness. After their exodus from Egypt, the Israelites faced a barren desert with no natural means of sustenance. Yet, God provided for them in miraculous ways.

For forty years, He sent manna from heaven, a daily provision of bread that sustained them. This heavenly food appeared each morning, and the Israelites were instructed to gather just enough for each day, except on the sixth day when they gathered twice as much to prepare for the Sabbath. This taught them to trust in God's daily provision and not to hoard out of fear of lack (Exodus 16:4-5).

Moreover, God provided water from a rock when they were desperately thirsty (Exodus 17:6). This act of provision was not just about quenching their physical thirst but was also a profound demonstration of His power and faithfulness. These stories underscore the principle that God's provision often comes in unexpected and miraculous ways, reinforcing the importance of trusting Him in every situation.

2. Elijah and the Ravens

In 1 Kings 17, we find the story of Elijah, who prophesied a severe drought in Israel. During this time, God instructed Elijah to hide by the Brook Cherith, where he would drink from the brook, and God commanded ravens to bring him food.

This narrative is extraordinary because ravens, by nature, do not share food—they are scavengers. Yet, under God's command, these birds brought Elijah bread and meat every morning and evening. This miracle demonstrates that God's provision can come from the most unlikely sources. It teaches believers that God's ways are higher than our ways, and His provision is not limited by natural circumstances.

3. The Widow of Zarephath

Continuing with Elijah's story, after the brook dried up, God directed him to a widow in Zarephath who was preparing her last meal for herself and her son before resigning to death by starvation. Elijah, following God's direction, asked her to make him a small cake first, promising that her jar of flour and jug of oil would not run dry until the Lord sent rain upon the land.

Despite her dire situation, the widow obeyed. True to the promise, her resources miraculously replenished daily (1 Kings 17:8-16). This story highlights the power of obedience and faith, showing that even in the midst of scarcity, God's provision can be abundant and continuous when we trust and obey His word.

4. Jesus Feeds the Five Thousand

In the New Testament, the miracle of Jesus feeding the five thousand with five loaves and two fish (Matthew 14:13-21) is a powerful testament to divine provision. Faced with a large, hungry crowd, the disciples saw only the insufficiency of their resources. However, Jesus took the small offering, gave thanks, and distributed it to the people. Miraculously, not only was everyone fed, but twelve baskets of leftovers were collected.

This miracle illustrates several key principles: God's ability to multiply what we offer Him, the importance of gratitude, and the abundance that follows divine intervention. It serves as a reminder that no matter how little we think we have, God can transform it into more than enough.

5. The Early Church and Acts of Generosity

In Acts 2:44-45 and Acts 4:32-37, we see the early church embodying a culture of divine provision through communal generosity. Believers shared their possessions and resources, ensuring that no one among them lacked anything. This was not merely human effort but a reflection of God's provision working through His people.

Barnabas, known as the "son of encouragement," sold a field he owned and brought the money to the apostles to help those in need. This act of generosity exemplified how God's provision often flows through the hands and hearts of those who follow Him, creating a community where His abundance is experienced collectively.

These biblical examples serve as profound reminders that God's provision is not just a historical occurrence but a living promise for believers today.

By studying these stories, we learn that divine provision often requires faith, obedience, and sometimes comes in the most unexpected ways. As Christians, we are called to trust in God's promises, knowing that He is our ultimate provider, capable of meeting all our needs according to His riches in glory (Philippians 4:19).

The Role of Faith in Financial Blessings

Faith plays an essential role in the Christian journey, especially when it comes to believing in God's promise of provision. The Bible is replete with instances where faith not only moved mountains but also unlocked the gates of divine provision.

Faith as the Foundation

At the heart of Christianity lies faith—a belief in the unseen and the assurance of things hoped for (Hebrews 11:1). This principle applies to all areas of life, including finances. Faith in God's provision means trusting that He is Jehovah-Jireh, our provider, who will meet all our needs according to His riches in glory (Philippians 4:19). This trust isn't passive but an active, dynamic belief that influences our thoughts, actions, and decisions regarding our resources.

Biblical Examples of Faith-Driven Provision

1. Elijah and the Widow at Zarephath (1 Kings 17:8-16): This story exemplifies how faith in God's word can lead to miraculous provision. Despite the famine, the widow believed Elijah's promise from God and used her last bit of flour and oil to bake bread for him. Her faith was rewarded with a continuous supply of food throughout the drought. This narrative underscores the principle that faith in God's directives can open the door to supernatural provision.

2. The Feeding of the 5,000 (Matthew 14:13-21): Jesus feeding five thousand men, besides women and children, with just five loaves of bread and two fish is a powerful illustration of divine multiplication through faith. When the disciples obeyed Jesus' instruction to distribute the meager supplies, their faith facilitated a miraculous increase. This event teaches that when we act in faith, God can multiply our resources beyond natural limitations.

Practical Steps to Strengthen Faith for Financial Blessings

1. Meditate on God's Promises: Regularly reading and meditating on scriptures about God's provision can strengthen your faith. Verses like Psalm 23:1, "The Lord is my shepherd; I shall not want," and Matthew 6:33, "But seek first his kingdom and his righteousness, and all these things will be given to you as well," are powerful reminders of God's promise to provide.

2. Declare God's Word: Speaking God's promises over your life can reinforce your faith. Positive confessions such as, "God is my provider, and I will not lack any good thing," align your words with God's truth, fostering a mindset of abundance.

3. Step Out in Faith: Faith requires action. This might mean giving generously even when it seems illogical, investing in opportunities that align with God's guidance, or simply trusting God's timing for financial breakthroughs. James 2:17 reminds us that faith without works is dead; our actions must reflect our belief in God's provision.

4. Pray with Expectation: Prayer is a vital component of faith. When you pray for financial blessings, do so with the expectation that God will answer. Mark 11:24 says, "Therefore I tell you, whatever you ask for in prayer, believe that you have received it, and it will be yours." Approach God with confidence, knowing He delights in providing for His children.

5. Cultivate a Grateful Heart: Gratitude shifts your focus from lack to abundance, reinforcing your faith in God's provision. Regularly thanking God for His blessings, both big and small, can build your faith muscle and create an atmosphere of expectation for more.

Challenges and Growth in Faith

It's important to acknowledge that faith is often tested in times of financial hardship. These seasons are opportunities for growth, teaching us to rely more deeply on God's provision. Remember, the testing of your faith produces perseverance (James 1:3), and perseverance leads to spiritual maturity. Embrace these challenges as divine appointments for greater blessings.

Faith is the currency of the Kingdom of God. It activates the promises of God and positions us to receive His financial blessings. By immersing ourselves in God's Word, declaring His promises, stepping out in faith, praying expectantly, and maintaining a heart of gratitude, we align ourselves with God's abundant provision. Let us boldly trust in Jehovah-Jireh, confident that poverty is not an option for those who walk by faith and not by sight.

Prayer and Provision: Seeking God's Help

Prayer is a fundamental aspect of the Christian faith, acting as a direct line of communication with God. When it comes to financial provision, prayer is not merely a ritual but a powerful tool to unlock the blessings that God has promised His children.

Understanding the Role of Prayer in Provision

Prayer is more than asking God for help; it's about building a relationship with Him. In the context of provision, prayer serves multiple purposes:

1. Acknowledgment of God's Sovereignty: When we pray for provision, we acknowledge that God is the ultimate source of all blessings. It's an act of humbling ourselves, recognizing that our efforts alone are insufficient without His intervention.

2. Expression of Faith: Prayer reflects our faith in God's promises. Hebrews 11:6 states, "And without faith, it is impossible to please God, because anyone who comes to him must believe that he exists and that he rewards those who earnestly seek him." Our prayers must be rooted in the belief that God is willing and able to provide.

3. Alignment with God's Will: Through prayer, we seek to align our desires with God's will. This alignment ensures that our requests are in harmony with His divine plans for our lives, leading to prayers that are more likely to be answered affirmatively.

Biblical Foundation for Prayer and Provision

The Bible is replete with examples and teachings about the power of prayer in accessing God's provision. Matthew 6:11, part of the Lord's Prayer, explicitly asks, "Give us today our daily bread." This simple yet profound request highlights the importance of daily dependence on God for our needs.

The Widow's Oil: A Lesson in Persistent Prayer

One of the most illustrative stories of prayer and provision is found in 2 Kings 4:1-7, where a widow, in desperate need, approached the prophet

Elisha. She had nothing but a small jar of oil. Elisha instructed her to gather as many empty vessels as she could and to pour oil into them. As she obeyed and prayed for God's intervention, the oil miraculously filled all the vessels, providing her with enough to pay her debts and live on the surplus. This story underscores the importance of obedience and faith in prayer, showing that God's provision often exceeds our expectations when we trust Him fully.

Developing a Powerful Prayer Life for Provision

To effectively seek God's help in financial matters, Christians must develop a robust prayer life. Here are key steps to cultivate such a prayer life:

- Consistency: Regular, daily prayer is crucial. It reflects a continual dependence on God and keeps us in constant communication with Him.
- Specificity: When praying for provision, be specific about your needs. Philippians 4:6 encourages us to present our requests to God. Specific prayers show that we trust God with the details of our lives.
- Gratitude: Begin and end your prayers with gratitude. Thanking God for past provisions strengthens our faith and opens our hearts to receive more.
- Scripture-Based Prayers: Use God's Word in your prayers. Remind Him of His promises. Scriptures like Philippians 4:19, "And my God

will meet all your needs according to the riches of his glory in Christ Jesus," are powerful declarations of faith.

Overcoming Hindrances to Effective Prayer

There are several factors that can hinder our prayers from being effective:

- Unconfessed Sin: Sin creates a barrier between us and God. Psalm 66:18 says, "If I had cherished sin in my heart, the Lord would not have listened." Regular confession and repentance are vital.
- Lack of Faith: James 1:6-7 warns against doubting when we pray. We must believe that God is willing and able to provide.
- Wrong Motives: James 4:3 highlights that asking with wrong motives can lead to unanswered prayers. Our desires should align with God's will and purposes.

The Power of Corporate Prayer

While personal prayer is crucial, corporate prayer—praying with others—also holds immense power. Matthew 18:19-20 states, "Again, truly I tell you that if two of you on earth agree about anything they ask for, it will be done for them by my Father in heaven. For where two or three gather in my name, there am I with them." Engaging in prayer with fellow believers can strengthen our faith and bring about miraculous provisions.

Boldly Approaching the Throne of Grace

Hebrews 4:16 encourages us to approach God's throne of grace with confidence, "so that we may receive mercy and find grace to help us in our time of need." This boldness comes from knowing that we are His children, and He delights in providing for us. By cultivating a life of consistent, faith-filled, and scripture-based prayer, we position ourselves to receive God's abundant provision, living out the truth that poverty is not an option for His children.

Testimonies of Miraculous Provision

In the journey of faith, testimonies serve as powerful reminders of God's unfailing provision and His ability to intervene supernaturally in our lives. The Bible is replete with stories of miraculous provision, each one illustrating God's care for His people and His desire to meet their needs abundantly. These testimonies are not just historical accounts; they are living examples that inspire us to trust God more deeply and expect His provision in our own lives.

1. The Widow of Zarephath: A Lesson in Faith and Obedience

One of the most striking testimonies of miraculous provision is found in the story of the widow of Zarephath (1 Kings 17:8-16). During a severe famine, God instructed the prophet Elijah to go to Zarephath, where a widow would provide for him. When Elijah arrived, he found the widow gathering sticks to prepare a final meal for herself and her son, fully expecting to die of starvation afterward. Despite her dire circumstances, Elijah asked her to first make a small cake for him, promising that God would provide for her needs. In an extraordinary act of faith and obedience, the widow complied, and the Bible records that her jar of flour and jug of oil did not run dry until the famine ended.

This story demonstrates the principle of giving out of lack and trusting in God's promise of provision. The widow's obedience opened the door for a continuous miracle, showcasing that even in the most desperate times, God can and will provide when we trust and obey Him.

2. The Feeding of the Five Thousand: Abundance in the Hands of Jesus

In the New Testament, the miracle of Jesus feeding the five thousand (John 6:1-14) is a profound example of divine provision. Faced with a massive crowd and limited resources—just five loaves of bread and two fish—Jesus performed a miracle of multiplication. After giving thanks, He distributed the food to the people, and everyone ate until they were satisfied. Remarkably, twelve baskets of leftovers were collected afterward, highlighting the superabundance of God's provision.

This event teaches us that no matter how limited our resources may seem, when placed in Jesus' hands, they can be multiplied to meet every need. It encourages believers to offer whatever they have to God, trusting Him to bring increase and provision far beyond human expectations.

3. Modern-Day Testimonies: God's Provision Continues

God's provision is not confined to the pages of the Bible; countless modern-day testimonies echo these ancient miracles, affirming that God still provides for His people in miraculous ways.

Story 1: Provision in the Wilderness

A missionary couple working in a remote part of Africa faced a dire situation when their food supplies ran out, and the next delivery was weeks away. With no human solution in sight, they gathered their team and prayed fervently for God's intervention. The very next day, a previously unknown local farmer arrived at their doorstep with a truckload of fresh produce, saying he felt compelled to bring them food. This unexpected and timely provision reminded the missionaries and their team that God hears and answers prayers, often through unexpected means.

Story 2: Financial Breakthrough

A Christian business owner was on the brink of bankruptcy. Despite faithful tithing and diligent work, financial pressures mounted, and creditors were closing in. In desperation, he sought God in prayer and received a word to sow a significant seed into another ministry. Obeying this difficult instruction, he gave what little he had left. Within days, a major contract that had been stalled for months was approved, bringing in more than enough revenue to save the business. This miraculous turnaround demonstrated the principle of sowing and reaping and God's faithfulness to His promises.

Living in Expectation of Miracles

Testimonies of miraculous provision serve to build our faith and encourage us to live in expectation of God's intervention. They remind us that God is not limited by our circumstances and that His resources are infinite. As believers, we are called to trust in God's promises, obey His instructions, and remain faithful in prayer and stewardship. By doing so, we position ourselves to experience His miraculous provision, just as the widow of Zarephath, the multitude fed by Jesus, and countless others have experienced throughout history.

The testimonies of miraculous provision in both biblical times and modern-day experiences affirm the truth that poverty is not an option for those who trust in God's divine provision. These stories inspire us to live with bold faith, expectant hearts, and unwavering confidence in the God who promises to supply all our needs according to His glorious riches in Christ Jesus (Philippians 4:19).

Chapter 2

Breaking the Chains of Poverty Mindset

Recognizing the Poverty Mindset

In the realm of Christian living, the battle against poverty is not merely a physical or financial struggle but a deeply spiritual one. The first and foremost step towards breaking free from the chains of poverty is recognizing and understanding the poverty mindset. This mindset, which is often ingrained through societal influences, personal experiences, and even cultural teachings, can significantly hinder one's ability to experience God's abundance.

The poverty mindset is characterized by a constant sense of lack, fear of scarcity, and a belief that financial struggle is an inevitable part of life. It is a mindset that says, "I will never have enough," "I am destined to be poor," or "Wealth is unattainable for someone like me." This way of thinking is not only limiting but is also contrary to the teachings of the Bible, which clearly outlines God's desire for His people to live in abundance and prosperity.

To recognize the poverty mindset, one must first acknowledge its subtle but powerful manifestations:

1. Fear of Scarcity: This is the fear that there will never be enough resources, whether it's money, food, or opportunities. It drives individuals to hoard, be overly cautious, and live in a state of constant anxiety. This fear is in direct opposition to the Biblical promise found in Philippians 4:19, "And my God will meet all your needs according to the riches of his glory in Christ Jesus."

2. Self-Sabotage: Often, individuals with a poverty mindset unconsciously sabotage their own success. This can be seen in decisions that lead to financial loss, missed opportunities, or not taking risks that could lead to prosperity. The Bible encourages believers to have a sound mind and make wise decisions (2 Timothy 1:7), indicating that self-sabotage is a deviation from God's plan.

3. Negative Confession: Words have power. Constantly speaking negatively about one's financial situation or declaring statements like "I can't afford this" or "I'll never get out of debt" reinforces the poverty mindset. Proverbs 18:21 states, "The tongue has the power of life and death," underscoring the importance of positive confession.

4. Entitlement and Dependency: This aspect of the poverty mindset is the belief that one is entitled to help or that someone else should be responsible for their financial well-being. While the Bible teaches about the importance of community and helping one another, it also emphasizes personal responsibility and hard work (2 Thessalonians 3:10).

5. Lack of Vision and Hope: Without a vision for the future, people perish (Proverbs 29:18). The poverty mindset often blinds individuals to the possibilities of a better future, causing them to settle for less and not strive for greater things.

Breaking Free from the Poverty Mindset

Recognizing these traits is just the beginning. To truly break free, a transformation of the mind is required, grounded in Biblical truths and principles. Romans 12:2 urges believers to be transformed by the renewing of their minds. Here are some practical steps to achieve this transformation:

- Embrace God's Promises: Immerse yourself in scriptures that speak of God's provision and abundance. Meditate on verses such as Jeremiah 29:11, which declares God's plans to prosper you, and Deuteronomy 8:18, which reminds us that it is God who gives us the ability to produce wealth.

- Renew Your Mind with Positive Confession: Replace negative statements with positive affirmations based on God's word. Speak life over your finances and believe in God's ability to provide. Declare daily, "God is my provider; I shall not want" (Psalm 23:1).

- Develop a Vision for Prosperity: Set clear, faith-filled goals for your financial future. Seek God's guidance in creating a vision that aligns with His will for your life. Remember, "Where there is no vision, the people perish" (Proverbs 29:18).

- Practice Gratitude and Generosity: Cultivate an attitude of gratitude for what you have, and practice generosity. Give to others and to the work of the Kingdom, knowing that God blesses a cheerful giver (2 Corinthians 9:7).

- Seek Wisdom and Counsel: Surround yourself with godly counsel and seek wisdom in financial matters. Proverbs 15:22 says, "Plans fail for lack of counsel, but with many advisers they succeed." Learn from those who have experienced financial freedom and apply their insights.

By recognizing and addressing the poverty mindset through these practical, faith-based strategies, believers can break free from financial bondage and step into the abundant life that God has promised. This transformation is not just about acquiring wealth but about living in the fullness of God's provision, peace, and purpose.

Renewing Your Mind with God's Truth

In the journey to overcoming poverty, renewing your mind with God's truth is a pivotal step. Romans 12:2 (NIV) instructs, "Do not conform to the pattern of this world, but be transformed by the renewing of your mind. Then you will be able to test and approve what God's will is—His good, pleasing and perfect will." This verse underscores the importance of transformation through mind renewal, which is foundational for breaking the chains of a poverty mindset.

A poverty mindset is a mental stronghold that convinces individuals they are destined for lack, scarcity, and financial struggle. It whispers lies that contradict God's promises of abundance and provision. This mindset is often rooted in past experiences, cultural teachings, and even generational curses. To break free, one must immerse their mind in the truth of God's Word, allowing it to dismantle these strongholds and replace them with His divine perspective.

1. Understanding the Root of Poverty Mindset

Before renewal can occur, it's crucial to understand the origins of a poverty mindset. Many people grow up in environments where financial struggle is normalized. Phrases like "money doesn't grow on trees" or "we can't afford that" become ingrained in their thinking. Additionally, societal influences and media often portray wealth as attainable only through dubious means or for a select few. These beliefs can become internalized, creating a subconscious barrier to financial prosperity.

2. The Power of God's Word

Hebrews 4:12 (NIV) states, "For the word of God is alive and active. Sharper than any double-edged sword, it penetrates even to dividing soul and spirit, joints and marrow; it judges the thoughts and attitudes of the heart." God's Word is powerful and transformative. To renew your mind, you must saturate it with Scripture that speaks to God's promises of provision and abundance. Verses such as Philippians 4:19 ("And my God will meet all your needs according to the riches of his glory in Christ Jesus") and Deuteronomy 28:12 ("The Lord will open the heavens, the storehouse of his bounty, to send rain on your land in season and to bless all the work of your hands") should be meditated upon and memorized.

3. Identifying and Rejecting Lies

A critical step in mind renewal is identifying the lies you have believed about money and rejecting them. For instance, the belief that "I will always be poor" is a lie that must be confronted with the truth of God's Word, such as Jeremiah 29:11 (NIV): "For I know the plans I have for you, declares the Lord, plans to prosper you and not to harm you, plans to give you hope and a future." Replace lies with truth by declaring Scriptures over your life daily. This practice not only breaks down the strongholds but also builds up your faith.

4. The Role of Positive Confession

Positive confession is a powerful tool in renewing your mind. Proverbs 18:21 (NIV) teaches, "The tongue has the power of life and death, and those who love it will eat its fruit." Speak life over your finances by declaring God's promises. Confess daily: "I am a child of God, and my Father owns the cattle on a thousand hills. I live in abundance and not in lack. My needs are met according to His glorious riches in Christ Jesus." These confessions align your thoughts and words with God's truth, paving the way for transformation.

5. Transforming Your Thought Patterns

Renewing your mind involves a continuous effort to align your thoughts with God's truth. Philippians 4:8 (NIV) provides a blueprint for this: "Finally, brothers and sisters, whatever is true, whatever is noble, whatever is right, whatever is pure, whatever is lovely, whatever is admirable—if anything is excellent or praiseworthy—think about such things." Replace negative, limiting thoughts with positive, faith-filled ones. When thoughts of lack arise, counter them with thoughts of God's provision and promises.

6. Embracing a Prosperity Mindset

To fully break free from a poverty mindset, embrace a prosperity mindset rooted in Scripture. This does not mean chasing material wealth for its own sake but understanding that God desires to bless you so you can be a blessing to others (Genesis 12:2-3). A prosperity mindset is about living in the overflow of God's blessings, having enough to meet your needs and plenty to share with others. It's about being a good steward of the resources God has entrusted to you and using them to further His kingdom.

7. Practical Steps for Mind Renewal

- Daily Devotionals: Spend time each day reading and meditating on Scriptures that speak to God's provision.
- Affirmations: Write down affirmations based on God's promises and declare them over your life.
- Journaling: Keep a journal of your journey, noting the Scriptures that speak to you and the progress you see.
- Community: Surround yourself with a faith-filled community that encourages and supports your journey.
- Prayer: Continually pray for God to renew your mind and reveal any lingering lies you may believe.

Renewing your mind with God's truth is a transformative process that requires dedication and faith. By immersing yourself in His Word, rejecting the lies of a poverty mindset, and embracing a prosperity mindset, you can break free from the chains of financial lack and walk in the abundance God has planned for you. Remember, poverty is not an option in God's kingdom, and He has already provided all that you need to live a life of fullness and prosperity.

The Power of Positive Confession

The words we speak hold immense power, shaping our reality and determining our destiny. In a Christian context, the power of positive confession is not merely about optimistic thinking but about aligning our speech with God's Word and His promises for our lives. Proverbs 18:21 tells us, "Death and life are in the power of the tongue, and those who love it will eat its fruit." This verse underscores the biblical principle that our words can either bring life or death, blessings or curses.

Biblical Foundation

The concept of positive confession is deeply rooted in the Bible. Throughout Scripture, we see the importance of speaking God's promises and truths over our lives. In Mark 11:23, Jesus says, "Truly I tell you, if anyone says to this mountain, 'Go, throw yourself into the sea,' and does not doubt in their heart but believes that what they say will happen, it will be done for them." This verse highlights the power of faith-filled words. When we confess God's promises, we activate our faith and align our circumstances with His will.

Another profound example is found in Romans 4:17, where Abraham is described as believing in "the God who gives life to the dead and calls into being things that were not." Abraham's positive confession of God's promises, despite his natural circumstances, resulted in the fulfillment of those promises. This teaches us that our words, when spoken in faith, can bring God's supernatural provision and blessings into our reality.

Practical Applications

1. Aligning Speech with Scripture: To harness the power of positive confession, we must first immerse ourselves in God's Word. By studying Scripture, we discover His promises regarding provision, abundance, and prosperity. Verses such as Philippians 4:19, "And my God will meet all your needs according to the riches of his glory in Christ Jesus," should be on our lips daily. Confessing these promises over our lives reaffirms our faith and expectation of God's provision.

2. Daily Affirmations: Developing a habit of daily affirmations rooted in Scripture can significantly impact our mindset. Start each day by declaring God's promises over your life. Statements like "I am blessed and highly favored" (Luke 1:28) and "The Lord is my Shepherd; I lack nothing" (Psalm 23:1) can transform our thinking and break the chains of a poverty mindset.

3. Rejecting Negative Speech: Just as positive words can bring life, negative words can reinforce a poverty mindset. We must be vigilant in rejecting negative speech about our finances, future, and identity. Avoid phrases like "I can't afford this" or "I'll never get out of debt." Instead, replace them with faith-filled declarations such as "God is my provider" and "I am more than a conqueror" (Romans 8:37).

4. Prayer and Confession: Incorporate positive confession into your prayer life. As you pray, speak God's promises back to Him. This not only strengthens your faith but also invites God's power into your situation. For example, praying, "Lord, I thank You that You supply all my needs according to Your riches in glory" (Philippians 4:19) reaffirms your trust in His provision.

5. Community and Accountability: Surround yourself with a community of believers who also practice positive confession. Share your declarations with them and hold each other accountable. Encourage one another with testimonies of how positive confession has brought about financial breakthroughs and blessings. This communal support reinforces the habit and mindset of speaking life.

Breaking the Chains of a Poverty Mindset

A poverty mindset is often reinforced by years of negative thinking and speaking. To break free, we must consciously and consistently replace those negative patterns with positive, faith-filled confessions. This transformation begins with recognizing the lies we've believed about our finances and replacing them with God's truth.

Consider the Israelites in the wilderness, who, despite seeing God's miraculous provision, often spoke negatively about their circumstances. Their complaints and lack of faith kept them wandering for forty years. In contrast, Caleb and Joshua, who spoke positively about God's ability to give them the Promised Land, were the only two from their generation to enter it (Numbers 14:30). Their positive confession and unwavering faith in God's promises set them apart and brought them into their inheritance.

The power of positive confession is a divine principle that can transform our lives and break the chains of a poverty mindset. By aligning our speech with God's Word, rejecting negative language, and consistently speaking life, we invite God's blessings and provision into our circumstances. Let us embrace the power of our words and, like Caleb and Joshua, speak faith and life into our financial situations, knowing that poverty is not an option when we walk in God's promises.

Developing a Prosperity Mindset

Developing a prosperity mindset is essential for Christians who seek to break free from the chains of a poverty mentality. This mindset is rooted in the belief that God desires His children to live abundantly and experience His blessings in every area of their lives, including finances. To cultivate a prosperity mindset, it is crucial to align our thoughts, words, and actions with the principles found in Scripture.

1. Recognize Your Identity in Christ

The foundation of a prosperity mindset begins with understanding our identity in Christ. As believers, we are children of the King, heirs to His promises, and recipients of His divine inheritance. Ephesians 1:3 states, "Blessed be the God and Father of our Lord Jesus Christ, who has blessed us in Christ with every spiritual blessing in the heavenly places." Recognizing that we are blessed and favored by God empowers us to expect His provision and abundance in our lives. This understanding shifts our perspective from scarcity to sufficiency, enabling us to walk confidently in God's promises.

2. Meditate on God's Promises

Meditation on God's Word is a powerful tool for transforming our minds. Joshua 1:8 instructs, "This Book of the Law shall not depart from your mouth, but you shall meditate on it day and night, so that you may be careful to do according to all that is written in it. For then you will make your way prosperous, and then you will have good success." By regularly meditating on Scriptures that speak of God's provision, abundance, and prosperity, we allow His truth to saturate our minds and hearts. Verses like Philippians 4:19, "And my God will supply every need of yours according to his riches in glory in Christ Jesus," remind us of God's unwavering faithfulness to provide for His children.

3. Speak Life and Blessings

The words we speak have tremendous power to shape our reality. Proverbs 18:21 declares, "Death and life are in the power of the tongue, and those who love it will eat its fruits." Developing a prosperity mindset involves intentionally speaking words of life, blessings, and abundance over ourselves and our circumstances. Instead of declaring lack or scarcity, we must align our speech with God's promises. Confessions such as "I am blessed and highly favored," "God is my provider," and "I walk in divine abundance" reinforce a mindset of prosperity and attract God's blessings into our lives.

4. Act in Faith and Obedience

Faith without works is dead (James 2:17). A prosperity mindset is not merely about positive thinking; it requires action rooted in faith and obedience to God's Word. This involves being diligent and hardworking, as Proverbs 10:4 states, "A slack hand causes poverty, but the hand of the diligent makes rich." It also includes practicing wise stewardship, tithing, and generous giving. Luke 6:38 promises, "Give, and it will be given to you. Good measure, pressed down, shaken together, running over, will be put into your lap. For with the measure you use it will be measured back to you." By stepping out in faith and obeying God's principles, we position ourselves to receive His supernatural provision and blessings.

5. Surround Yourself with Faith-filled Influences

Our environment and the people we associate with can significantly impact our mindset. Proverbs 13:20 advises, "Whoever walks with the wise becomes wise, but the companion of fools will suffer harm." To develop a prosperity mindset, it is essential to surround ourselves with faith-filled influences—people who encourage us, speak life, and share our belief in God's provision. Engaging in a community of like-minded believers who inspire and challenge us to grow in faith fosters an atmosphere of expectancy and reinforces our commitment to a prosperity mindset.

6. Cultivate a Heart of Gratitude

Gratitude is a powerful attitude that attracts God's blessings. 1 Thessalonians 5:18 instructs, "Give thanks in all circumstances; for this is the will of God in Christ Jesus for you." Cultivating a heart of gratitude involves acknowledging and appreciating God's goodness, even in challenging times. By focusing on what we have rather than what we lack, we shift our perspective to one of abundance. Regularly expressing gratitude to God for His provision, both big and small, keeps our hearts aligned with His promises and opens the door for more blessings to flow into our lives.

Developing a prosperity mindset is a transformative journey that requires intentionality, faith, and a deep reliance on God's Word. By recognizing our identity in Christ, meditating on His promises, speaking life and blessings, acting in faith and obedience, surrounding ourselves with positive influences, and cultivating gratitude, we can break free from the chains of a poverty mentality and walk in the fullness of God's provision. Remember, poverty is not an option for God's children. He has called us to live abundantly, reflecting His glory and advancing His Kingdom on earth. Embrace the prosperity mindset and step into the divine abundance that God has prepared for you.

Overcoming Fear and Doubt

Fear and doubt are two of the most significant barriers that prevent believers from experiencing the fullness of God's financial blessings. These mental strongholds can paralyze our faith, diminish our confidence, and ultimately hinder us from stepping into the abundant life that God has promised.

The Origin of Fear and Doubt

Fear and doubt are not of God. The Bible clearly states in 2 Timothy 1:7, "For God has not given us a spirit of fear, but of power and of love and of a sound mind." These negative emotions often originate from past experiences, negative words spoken over our lives, or even societal influences that suggest scarcity and lack. The enemy uses these emotions to keep us bound and ineffective, preventing us from accessing God's promises.

The Impact of Fear and Doubt on Financial Prosperity

When fear and doubt take root, they create a mindset of scarcity. This mindset leads to poor financial decisions, such as hoarding resources, avoiding investments, or refusing to step out in faith when God calls us to give or start something new. Proverbs 23:7 says, "For as he thinks in his heart, so is he." Our thoughts shape our reality. If we believe in scarcity, we will live in scarcity, despite the abundance God has in store for us.

Biblical Examples of Overcoming Fear and Doubt

The Bible is replete with stories of individuals who overcame fear and doubt to receive God's blessings. Consider the story of Gideon in Judges 6-7. Gideon was initially fearful and doubted his ability to lead Israel against the Midianites. However, God reassured him with His presence and promises. Gideon's faith grew, and he eventually led a small army to a miraculous victory, demonstrating that overcoming fear and doubt can lead to divine success.

Another example is Peter walking on water in Matthew 14:22-33. Peter began to sink when he shifted his focus from Jesus to the storm around him. This illustrates how fear and doubt can cause us to falter. Yet, when Peter cried out to Jesus, he was saved, emphasizing the importance of focusing on God rather than our circumstances.

Strategies for Overcoming Fear and Doubt

1. Renewing the Mind: Romans 12:2 instructs us to be transformed by the renewing of our minds. This involves replacing negative thoughts with God's promises. Memorize and meditate on scriptures that affirm God's

provision, such as Philippians 4:19, "And my God will meet all your needs according to the riches of his glory in Christ Jesus."

2. Confession of Faith: Speak life over your finances. Proverbs 18:21 says, "Death and life are in the power of the tongue." Declare God's promises daily. For instance, say, "I am blessed and highly favored. God is my provider, and I lack nothing."

3. Stepping Out in Faith: Faith without works is dead (James 2:17). Act on God's word even when fear and doubt try to hold you back. This could mean starting a new venture, giving generously, or investing in opportunities that align with God's leading.

4. Seeking Godly Counsel: Proverbs 15:22 states, "Plans fail for lack of counsel, but with many advisers, they succeed." Surround yourself with believers who have strong faith and have experienced God's financial blessings. Their testimonies and guidance can help strengthen your faith.

5. Prayer and Fasting: Some breakthroughs require intensified spiritual discipline. Jesus said in Matthew 17:21, "This kind does not go out except by prayer and fasting." Commit to seeking God through prayer and fasting to break the chains of fear and doubt.

Living in God's Confidence

Living free from fear and doubt involves continually trusting in God's character and promises. It is a daily decision to walk in faith, knowing that God is faithful to His word. Psalm 34:4 says, "I sought the Lord, and he answered me; he delivered me from all my fears." Trusting God involves surrendering our worries to Him and believing that He will lead us into abundance.

Overcoming fear and doubt is crucial for breaking the poverty mindset. By renewing our minds, confessing faith, stepping out in faith, seeking godly counsel, and committing to prayer and fasting, we can align ourselves with God's plan for prosperity. Remember, God has not given us a spirit of fear. Embrace His promises, live boldly, and watch as He transforms your financial life beyond what you could ever imagine.

Chapter 3

Stewardship: Managing God's Resources

Biblical Principles of Stewardship

Stewardship is a fundamental concept in Christianity, embodying the idea that everything we have is entrusted to us by God and that we are responsible for managing these resources wisely. This principle is deeply rooted in the Bible, with numerous scriptures offering guidance on how to be effective stewards of the blessings we receive.

The Bible opens with a powerful example of stewardship in the Book of Genesis. God creates the world and entrusts Adam and Eve with the care of the Garden of Eden (Genesis 2:15). This act of entrusting humanity with His creation sets the precedent for all subsequent teachings on stewardship. It highlights the belief that God is the ultimate owner of all things, and we are merely caretakers, tasked with managing His resources.

Recognizing God as the Ultimate Owner

One of the foundational principles of biblical stewardship is the recognition that God is the owner of everything. Psalm 24:1 states, "The earth is the Lord's, and everything in it, the world, and all who live in it."

This verse emphasizes that everything we possess – our money, time, talents, and even our very lives – belongs to God. Understanding this helps us approach our responsibilities with humility and a sense of divine purpose.

Faithfulness in Small Things

In Luke 16:10, Jesus teaches, "Whoever can be trusted with very little can also be trusted with much, and whoever is dishonest with very little will also be dishonest with much." This principle underscores the importance of being faithful in managing even the smallest of resources. By demonstrating responsibility and integrity in small matters, we show God that we can be trusted with greater blessings. This approach fosters a culture of excellence and accountability in all aspects of life.

The Parable of the Talents

One of the most profound teachings on stewardship comes from the Parable of the Talents (Matthew 25:14-30). In this parable, a master entrusts his servants with different amounts of money, or "talents," before leaving on a journey. Upon his return, he assesses how each servant managed the resources. The servants who invested and multiplied their talents were rewarded, while the one who buried his talent out of fear was reprimanded and cast out.

This parable highlights several key aspects of stewardship:

- Accountability: Each servant had to account for how they managed the master's resources, reflecting the biblical truth that we will all give an account to God for how we managed what He entrusted to us (Romans 14:12).
- Initiative and Diligence: The servants who actively worked to multiply their talents were praised. This teaches us that God values initiative, hard work, and the willingness to take risks for His glory.
- Fear vs. Faith: The fearful servant buried his talent, demonstrating a lack of trust in the master. This serves as a caution against letting fear prevent us from using our gifts and resources effectively. Instead, we should operate in faith, trusting that God will guide and bless our efforts.

Generosity as a Cornerstone of Stewardship

Biblical stewardship is not just about managing resources but also about being generous. Proverbs 11:24-25 states, "One person gives freely, yet gains even more; another withholds unduly, but comes to poverty. A generous person will prosper; whoever refreshes others will be refreshed." This principle teaches that generosity is a key to unlocking God's blessings. By giving freely and joyfully, we reflect God's own generosity towards us and open ourselves to greater prosperity.

Practical Application of Stewardship Principles

To put these biblical principles into practice, consider the following steps:

1. Evaluate Your Resources: Take stock of everything God has entrusted to you – finances, talents, time, and relationships. Reflect on how you can manage these resources more effectively for His glory.
2. Set Goals and Priorities: Establish clear, godly goals for your resources. Prioritize activities and investments that align with biblical values and advance God's kingdom.
3. Be Accountable: Find an accountability partner or group to help you stay on track with your stewardship goals. Regularly review your progress and make adjustments as needed.
4. Cultivate Generosity: Make generosity a regular part of your life. Look for opportunities to bless others with your time, talents, and treasures. Trust that God will honor your generosity and provide for your needs.
5. Pray for Wisdom: Continuously seek God's guidance and wisdom in managing His resources. Pray for a heart that is aligned with His will and for the courage to act in faith.

Biblical stewardship is about recognizing God's ownership, being faithful with what we have, and cultivating a spirit of generosity. By embracing these principles, we not only honor God but also position ourselves to experience His abundant blessings. Stewardship is not a one-time act but a lifelong commitment to managing God's resources in a way that brings glory to Him and benefits others.

The Parable of the Talents: Lessons in Management

The Parable of the Talents, found in Matthew 25:14-30, is one of the most profound teachings of Jesus on the subject of stewardship and resource management. In this parable, a master entrusts his servants with different amounts of money, referred to as talents, before going on a journey. Each servant receives talents according to their ability: one receives five talents, another two, and another one. The master's return and his evaluation of the servants' management of the talents form the crux of the lesson.

The Trust of the Master

The first lesson from this parable is the trust the master places in his servants. This trust reflects God's trust in us as His stewards. God entrusts each of us with resources, talents, and opportunities according to our abilities. It is a profound privilege and responsibility to manage what He has given us wisely. The master did not give his servants the same amount, acknowledging that each person has different capacities and strengths. Similarly, God recognizes our individual potential and equips us accordingly.

Faithfulness in Management

The servants who received five and two talents immediately went to work and doubled their master's money. This action signifies diligence, initiative, and the understanding that they were accountable for their stewardship. These servants demonstrated faithfulness, an essential quality God seeks in His stewards. Faithfulness involves using what we have been given to its fullest potential, regardless of the quantity. It means being proactive, industrious, and responsible.

The servant who received one talent, however, chose to bury it in the ground. This act was a failure of stewardship. He allowed fear, insecurity, and perhaps laziness to dictate his actions. This servant's behavior teaches us that failing to utilize our resources and talents is a significant mismanagement of what God has entrusted to us. God expects us to grow and expand what we have, not to hide it out of fear or negligence.

Accountability and Reward

Upon the master's return, he settled accounts with his servants. The servants who had doubled their talents were commended for their good and faithful stewardship and were rewarded with greater responsibilities and joy. "Well done, good and faithful servant. You have been faithful over a few things; I will make you ruler over many things. Enter into the joy of your lord" (Matthew 25:21, 23). This commendation underscores the principle that faithfulness in small matters leads to greater opportunities and rewards. God honors and promotes those who manage their resources well.

In contrast, the servant who buried his talent was reprimanded and his talent was taken away and given to the servant who had ten talents. The master called him wicked and lazy, highlighting that doing nothing with what we have been given is inexcusable. This servant's punishment serves as a stark warning about the consequences of poor stewardship. It emphasizes that God expects us to be active and productive with the resources and talents He provides.

Application in Modern Christian Life

Applying the lessons from this parable to our modern Christian lives involves several practical steps:

1. Recognize and Acknowledge Your Talents and Resources: Understand that everything you have is a gift from God. Identify your unique talents, abilities, and resources and acknowledge them as tools for God's work.

2. Be Diligent and Proactive: Like the faithful servants, take initiative to improve and multiply what you have. Whether it's your finances, skills, or time, use them actively to benefit God's kingdom and others around you.

3. Overcome Fear and Inaction: The servant who buried his talent acted out of fear. Trust in God's provision and guidance, and do not let fear paralyze you from taking bold steps of faith.

4. Seek Continuous Improvement: Strive for growth and excellence in all you do. Be faithful in small tasks and seek ways to expand and enhance your impact.

5. Prepare for Accountability: Remember that one day, you will give an account to God for how you managed His resources. Let this accountability motivate you to be a good and faithful steward.

6. Celebrate and Share Success: When you achieve success through faithful stewardship, give glory to God and share your blessings with others. Your success should serve as a testimony of God's goodness and inspire others to manage their resources well.

The Parable of the Talents is not merely a story about money but a profound lesson about life, faithfulness, and accountability. As Christians, we are called to be diligent stewards, using our God-given resources wisely and effectively to further His kingdom and honor Him. In doing so, we align ourselves with God's will, experience His blessings, and ultimately hear those cherished words, "Well done, good and faithful servant."

Tithing and Offering: Keys to Blessing

Tithing and offering are fundamental principles in Christian stewardship, deeply rooted in the Bible and essential for experiencing God's blessings.

These practices, though sometimes misunderstood, are powerful acts of obedience and faith that unlock God's provision and favor.

The Biblical Foundation of Tithing

The concept of tithing, giving one-tenth of one's income, dates back to the Old Testament. The first mention of tithing is found in Genesis 14:18-20, where Abram (later Abraham) gives a tenth of everything to Melchizedek, the king of Salem and priest of God Most High. This act of giving was not mandated by law but was a voluntary expression of gratitude and reverence towards God.

Later, tithing became a formal requirement under the Mosaic Law. Leviticus 27:30 states, "A tithe of everything from the land, whether grain from the soil or fruit from the trees, belongs to the Lord; it is holy to the Lord." The tithe was a way for the Israelites to acknowledge God as the source of their provision and to support the Levitical priesthood, the temple, and the needs of the community.

In the New Testament, Jesus affirms the practice of tithing. In Matthew 23:23, He rebukes the Pharisees for their hypocritical legalism but acknowledges that tithing should not be neglected: "Woe to you, teachers of the law and Pharisees, you hypocrites! You give a tenth of your spices—mint, dill, and cumin. But you have neglected the more important matters of the law—justice, mercy, and faithfulness. You should have practiced the latter, without neglecting the former."

Offering: Beyond the Tithe

While tithing represents a specific portion, offerings are gifts given above and beyond the tithe. They are voluntary and come from a heart of generosity and gratitude. Offerings can take many forms, including monetary gifts, acts of service, or other resources.

The Bible is replete with examples of sacrificial offerings. One notable example is the widow's offering in Mark 12:41-44. Jesus observes a poor widow who puts two small copper coins into the temple treasury. Though her gift is monetarily small, Jesus declares it as greater than the large sums given by the rich because she gave all she had out of her poverty.

Paul also encourages generous giving in 2 Corinthians 9:6-7: "Remember this: Whoever sows sparingly will also reap sparingly, and whoever sows generously will also reap generously. Each of you should give what you have decided in your heart to give, not reluctantly or under compulsion, for God loves a cheerful giver." This passage underscores that offerings should be given willingly and joyfully, reflecting the giver's heart rather than the amount.

The Spiritual Impact of Tithing and Offering

Tithing and offering are not merely financial transactions but profound spiritual practices that shape a believer's relationship with God and their understanding of His provision. Here are some key spiritual impacts:

1. Acknowledgment of God's Sovereignty: Tithing acknowledges that everything we have comes from God. It is an act of worship, recognizing His lordship over our lives and resources.

2. Cultivating Trust and Dependence: Regularly giving a portion of our income to God fosters trust in His provision. It requires faith, especially when finances are tight, and teaches us to rely on God's faithfulness rather than our own understanding.

3. Breaking the Power of Materialism: In a world driven by consumerism, tithing and offering break the grip of materialism. By prioritizing God in our finances, we declare that our security and identity are found in Him, not in wealth or possessions.

4. Experiencing God's Blessings: Malachi 3:10 contains a unique promise: "Bring the whole tithe into the storehouse, that there may be food in my house. Test me in this," says the Lord Almighty, "and see if I will not throw open the floodgates of heaven and pour out so much blessing that there will not be room enough to store it." God invites us to test Him in this area, promising abundant blessings in response to faithful tithing.

5. Enabling Kingdom Work: Tithes and offerings fund the work of the church and the spread of the Gospel. They support pastors, missionaries, and various ministries, extending God's love and truth to a hurting world.

Practical Application: How to Tithe and Give Offerings

1. Set Aside the First Fruits: Tithing should be the first financial commitment made with each income, not an afterthought. This practice, known as giving the "first fruits," honors God with our best and acknowledges His provision.

2. Plan and Budget: Incorporate tithing and offerings into your financial planning. Create a budget that prioritizes giving, ensuring that it remains a consistent and intentional act of worship.

3. Pray for Guidance: Seek God's guidance in your giving. Ask Him to reveal opportunities to bless others and to use your resources for His glory.

4. Be Accountable: Share your commitment to tithing and offering with a trusted friend or mentor. Accountability can provide encouragement and support in maintaining your giving practices.

5. Celebrate Generosity: Reflect on the impact of your giving and celebrate the ways God uses your resources to further His kingdom.

Share testimonies of God's provision and the joy of generosity with others.

Tithing and offering are foundational practices for Christians seeking to live in obedience and experience God's blessings. They are acts of faith that acknowledge God's sovereignty, cultivate trust, break materialism, release blessings, and enable kingdom work. By embracing these principles, believers can walk in financial freedom and witness the miraculous provision of God in their lives.

Financial Planning and Budgeting

Financial planning and budgeting are critical components of stewardship, essential for Christians seeking to manage God's resources wisely. This section delves into the principles and practical steps for effective financial planning and budgeting, grounded in biblical wisdom and faith.

The Foundation of Financial Planning

Financial planning begins with understanding that all resources belong to God. Psalm 24:1 declares, "The earth is the Lord's, and everything in it, the world, and all who live in it." Recognizing God's ownership transforms our perspective on money, shifting our role to that of stewards entrusted with His resources. Proverbs 21:5 says, "The plans of the diligent lead surely to abundance, but everyone who is hasty comes only to poverty."

Planning is not just a practical step; it is a biblical mandate for achieving financial stability and growth.

Setting Financial Goals

A crucial aspect of financial planning is setting clear, God-honoring financial goals. These goals should reflect our values, priorities, and faith. Goals might include saving for a child's education, buying a home, supporting missions, or planning for retirement. Philippians 4:19 reassures us, "And my God will meet all your needs according to the riches of his glory in Christ Jesus." With faith, we set our goals, trusting God to provide the necessary resources.

When setting financial goals, it is vital to differentiate between needs and wants. Needs are essential for our well-being and fulfillment of our responsibilities, while wants are desires that may not be necessary. This discernment is guided by seeking God's wisdom through prayer and Scripture.

Creating a Budget

A budget is a detailed plan that outlines expected income and expenditures over a specific period. It serves as a roadmap for managing money and achieving financial goals. Luke 14:28-30 illustrates the importance of budgeting: "Suppose one of you wants to build a tower. Won't you first sit down and estimate the cost to see if you have enough money to complete it?"

To create an effective budget:

- Track Income and Expenses: Begin by documenting all sources of income and expenses. This includes salary, business income, tithes, offerings, bills, groceries, and discretionary spending. Tools like spreadsheets or budgeting apps can simplify this process.

- Categorize Spending: Divide expenses into categories such as housing, transportation, food, entertainment, and savings. This helps in identifying areas where spending can be adjusted.

- Allocate Funds: Assign a portion of income to each category based on priorities and goals. Ensure that essential needs and tithing are prioritized.

- Monitor and Adjust: Regularly review the budget to track progress and make necessary adjustments. Life changes and unexpected expenses may require reallocation of funds.

Saving and Investing

Proverbs 21:20 teaches, "The wise store up choice food and olive oil, but fools gulp theirs down." Saving and investing are prudent practices that prepare for future needs and opportunities. Savings provide a safety net for emergencies, while investments can grow wealth over time.

- Emergency Fund: Aim to save at least three to six months' worth of living expenses. This fund acts as a buffer against financial emergencies like job loss or medical expenses.

- Short-term and Long-term Savings: Identify short-term savings goals (e.g., vacation, new appliance) and long-term goals (e.g., retirement, home purchase). Allocate a portion of income to these goals consistently.

- Wise Investments: Invest in instruments that align with your risk tolerance and financial goals. Seek godly counsel and consider ethical investments that honor God's principles.

Generosity and Giving

Generosity is a vital aspect of Christian financial stewardship. 2 Corinthians 9:7 encourages, "Each of you should give what you have decided in your heart to give, not reluctantly or under compulsion, for God loves a cheerful giver." Incorporate giving into the budget, prioritizing tithes and offerings. Supporting church ministries, missions, and charitable causes reflects our trust in God's provision and our commitment to His kingdom work.

Financial planning and budgeting, when done with a heart aligned to God's will, become acts of worship and faithfulness. By diligently planning, setting goals, creating a budget, saving, investing, and giving generously, Christians can manage God's resources effectively, honoring Him in all financial decisions. This stewardship not only leads to financial stability but also glorifies God, demonstrating trust in His provision and commitment to His kingdom.

Giving Generously: The Heart of Stewardship

In the realm of Christian stewardship, giving generously is not merely a financial transaction; it is a profound spiritual discipline that mirrors the very heart of God. To understand this, we must delve deep into the biblical principles that underscore the essence of generosity and how it reflects our relationship with the Creator.

The Biblical Mandate for Generosity

The Bible is replete with exhortations to give generously. One of the most powerful scriptures is found in 2 Corinthians 9:6-7, where the Apostle Paul writes, "Remember this: Whoever sows sparingly will also reap sparingly, and whoever sows generously will also reap generously. Each of you should give what you have decided in your heart to give, not reluctantly or under compulsion, for God loves a cheerful giver." This passage highlights several key elements: the principle of sowing and reaping, the importance of intentional giving, and the joy that comes from giving.

Generosity is not about the amount given but the heart with which it is given. The widow's offering of two small coins in Mark 12:41-44 exemplifies this truth. Jesus commended her because she gave out of her poverty, all she had to live on, demonstrating that true generosity is sacrificial and trustful.

Generosity as a Reflection of God's Nature

God is the ultimate giver. John 3:16 declares, "For God so loved the world that he gave his one and only Son, that whoever believes in him shall not perish but have eternal life." God's giving is rooted in love and is the greatest example of generosity. When we give, we are reflecting His nature. Ephesians 5:1-2 urges us to be imitators of God and live a life of love, just as Christ loved us and gave himself up for us.

The Spiritual Benefits of Generosity

Generous giving has profound spiritual benefits. It breaks the power of materialism and greed in our lives. Jesus taught in Matthew 6:24 that we cannot serve both God and money. Generosity reorients our hearts towards God and away from the deceitful allure of wealth. It is a tangible way to lay up treasures in heaven, as Jesus advised in Matthew 6:19-21.

Moreover, giving generously fosters a deep sense of community and interdependence within the body of Christ. Acts 2:44-45 paints a picture of the early church where believers shared everything they had, ensuring that no one was in need. This radical generosity was a powerful testimony to the surrounding world of the transformative power of the gospel.

Practical Ways to Practice Generosity

- Tithing: The principle of tithing, giving 10% of one's income to the church, is a starting point for many believers. Malachi 3:10 promises blessings to those who faithfully tithe, "Bring the whole tithe into the storehouse, that there may be food in my house. Test me in this," says the LORD Almighty, "and see if I will not throw open the floodgates of heaven and pour out so much blessing that there will not be room enough to store it."

- Offerings: Beyond tithing, offerings are gifts given out of gratitude and a desire to support various ministries and causes. 2 Corinthians 9:8 emphasizes that God provides abundantly so that we can abound in every good work.

- Almsgiving: This involves giving directly to those in need. Proverbs 19:17 states, "Whoever is kind to the poor lends to the LORD, and he will reward them for what they have done." Almsgiving is a direct way to demonstrate God's love and compassion to the less fortunate.

- Supporting Missions: Investing in the spread of the gospel is another powerful form of generosity. Philippians 4:15-19 commends the church for supporting Paul's missionary work and assures them that God will meet all their needs according to His glorious riches in Christ Jesus.

- Legacy Giving: Consider leaving a portion of your estate to Christian ministries or charities. This ensures that your resources continue to advance God's kingdom even after your lifetime.

Cultivating a Heart of Generosity

Generosity begins in the heart. To cultivate a heart of generosity, we must continually renew our minds with God's Word. Meditate on scriptures that emphasize giving and God's provision. Pray for a spirit of generosity and look for opportunities to give. Engage with stories of generosity, both from the Bible and contemporary examples, to inspire and challenge your own giving.

Furthermore, it is essential to practice gratitude. Recognizing God's blessings in our lives fosters a spirit of thankfulness and a desire to bless others. Keeping a gratitude journal can help maintain this perspective.

Giving generously is at the heart of Christian stewardship. It reflects God's nature, brings spiritual benefits, and advances His kingdom. As we embrace a lifestyle of generosity, we not only obey God's commands but also experience the joy and fulfillment that comes from being His hands and feet in a world in need.

Chapter 4

The Power of Work and Diligence

The Biblical View of Work

The concept of work is deeply rooted in the Christian faith, tracing back to the very beginning of creation. In the book of Genesis, God Himself is depicted as the ultimate worker, creating the heavens and the earth in six days and resting on the seventh. This divine act sets a precedent for humanity, establishing work as a fundamental aspect of our existence and purpose.

The Theology of Work

Work is not a result of the Fall, but rather an integral part of God's original plan for humanity. Genesis 2:15 states, "The Lord God took the man and put him in the Garden of Eden to work it and take care of it." This verse reveals that work was assigned to Adam before sin entered the world, signifying that work is inherently good and purposeful. It is a means through which we can fulfill God's mandate to steward and cultivate the earth.

Moreover, the Bible portrays work as a reflection of God's character. In John 5:17, Jesus says, "My Father is always at his work to this very day, and I too am working." By engaging in work, we emulate the diligence and creativity of our Creator. This perspective transforms work from a mere obligation to a divine vocation, where every task, no matter how mundane, can be an act of worship.

Work as a Means of Provision

One of the primary purposes of work is to provide for ourselves and our families. The Apostle Paul emphasizes this in 1 Timothy 5:8, stating, "Anyone who does not provide for their relatives, and especially for their own household, has denied the faith and is worse than an unbeliever." This admonition underscores the importance of responsibility and diligence in our labor.

Additionally, Proverbs 14:23 asserts, "All hard work brings a profit, but mere talk leads only to poverty." This wisdom literature reinforces the principle that diligent work leads to tangible rewards, whereas idle talk and laziness result in lack. Therefore, the biblical view of work is inherently tied to the principles of provision and prosperity.

The Value of Diligence

The Bible is replete with exhortations to be diligent and industrious. Proverbs 12:24 declares, "Diligent hands will rule, but laziness ends in forced labor." This verse highlights the correlation between diligence and leadership, suggesting that those who work diligently are more likely to rise to positions of influence and authority.

Furthermore, Colossians 3:23-24 advises, "Whatever you do, work at it with all your heart, as working for the Lord, not for human masters, since you know that you will receive an inheritance from the Lord as a reward. It is the Lord Christ you are serving." This passage elevates the nature of work by positioning it as service to God, thereby infusing every occupation with spiritual significance.

Work and Rest: The Balance

While the Bible advocates for hard work, it also recognizes the necessity of rest. The concept of Sabbath, introduced in Genesis 2:2-3 and reiterated throughout Scripture, is a testament to God's understanding of the human need for rest. Exodus 20:8-10 commands, "Remember the Sabbath day by keeping it holy. Six days you shall labor and do all your work, but the seventh day is a sabbath to the Lord your God. On it you shall not do any work."

This balance between work and rest is crucial for holistic well-being. It prevents burnout and ensures that we remain effective and productive in our labor. By adhering to this divine rhythm, we honor God's design for our lives and acknowledge our dependence on His provision and sustenance.

Work as a Witness

Finally, our attitude towards work can serve as a powerful witness to those around us. In Titus 2:7-8, Paul instructs, "In everything set them an example by doing what is good. In your teaching show integrity, seriousness and soundness of speech that cannot be condemned, so that those who oppose you may be ashamed because they have nothing bad to say about us." Our diligence, integrity, and excellence in the workplace can reflect Christ's character and draw others to Him.

The biblical view of work is multifaceted, encompassing themes of divine reflection, provision, diligence, balance, and witness. By understanding and embracing this perspective, we can transform our approach to work from a mundane necessity to a meaningful vocation that glorifies God and fulfills His purpose for our lives. Let us, therefore, commit to working with excellence, diligence, and a heart of worship, knowing that in doing so, we serve the Lord Christ.

The Rewards of Hard Work and Diligence

The Bible is replete with teachings that extol the virtues of hard work and diligence. These principles are not just moral obligations but divine mandates that carry profound rewards both in this life and the next.

Understanding and embracing this can transform our approach to work, turning it from a mere necessity into a form of worship that honors God.

Biblical Foundations of Hard Work

From the very beginning, God established work as a fundamental aspect of human existence. In Genesis 2:15, we read that "The Lord God took the man and put him in the Garden of Eden to work it and take care of it." This verse illustrates that work was part of God's original plan for humanity. It wasn't a result of the Fall but a purposeful, meaningful activity designed by God.

The Book of Proverbs, known for its practical wisdom, repeatedly highlights the benefits of hard work and the consequences of laziness. Proverbs 10:4 states, "Lazy hands make for poverty, but diligent hands bring wealth." This clear dichotomy between diligence and laziness sets the stage for understanding the rewards of hard work.

Spiritual and Material Rewards

Hard work and diligence are not merely about earning a living or achieving material success. They are about aligning oneself with God's principles and experiencing His blessings. The rewards of hard work are manifold, encompassing spiritual growth, material prosperity, and personal fulfillment.

1. Spiritual Growth: Hard work is a form of stewardship of the gifts and talents God has given us. When we work diligently, we are using our God-given abilities to their fullest potential. Colossians 3:23-24 instructs us, "Whatever you do, work at it with all your heart, as working for the Lord, not for human masters, since you know that you will receive an inheritance from the Lord as a reward. It is the Lord Christ you are serving." This perspective transforms work into a spiritual exercise, fostering growth in character, discipline, and faith.

2. Material Prosperity: While the primary motivation for hard work should be to honor God, the Bible also promises material rewards. Proverbs 12:14 says, "From the fruit of their lips people are filled with good things, and the work of their hands brings them reward." God blesses those who are diligent and faithful in their work. This doesn't mean we will all become wealthy, but that our needs will be met, and we will experience God's provision in our lives.

3. Personal Fulfillment: There is an intrinsic satisfaction that comes from completing a task well done. Ecclesiastes 2:24-25 tells us, "A person can do nothing better than to eat and drink and find satisfaction in their own toil. This too, I see, is from the hand of God, for without him, who can eat or find enjoyment?" This satisfaction is a gift from God, a reward for our labor and diligence.

Diligence: The Path to Excellence

Diligence is more than just hard work; it is consistent, careful, and persistent effort. It requires patience, perseverance, and attention to detail. The Bible commends those who are diligent in their work, promising them success and recognition. Proverbs 22:29 declares, "Do you see someone skilled in their work? They will serve before kings; they will not serve before officials of low rank."

Diligence also protects us from the pitfalls of laziness and complacency. Proverbs 13:4 warns, "A sluggard's appetite is never filled, but the desires of the diligent are fully satisfied." By being diligent, we ensure that we are constantly progressing, improving, and achieving the goals set before us.

Practical Application

To experience the rewards of hard work and diligence, it is essential to adopt a mindset that values these principles. Here are practical steps to cultivate diligence:

1. Set Clear Goals: Establish clear, achievable goals that align with God's purpose for your life. Having a vision provides direction and motivation.

2. Develop a Strong Work Ethic: Commit to doing your best in every task, no matter how small. Remember, you are working for the Lord.

3. Stay Disciplined: Avoid distractions and remain focused on your tasks. Discipline is key to maintaining diligence over the long term.

4. Seek God's Guidance: Pray for wisdom and strength to carry out your work. Depend on God's power, not just your own abilities.

5. Reflect and Improve: Regularly evaluate your work and seek ways to improve. Learning from mistakes and striving for excellence are marks of diligence.

The rewards of hard work and diligence are both tangible and intangible, encompassing spiritual growth, material provision, and personal satisfaction. By embracing these principles, we align ourselves with God's design and open the door to His blessings. As we work diligently, we not only fulfill our responsibilities but also reflect God's glory in our lives, serving as a testimony to His faithfulness and provision. Remember, poverty is not an option when we diligently apply ourselves to the work God has set before us, trusting in His promises and provision.

Avoiding Laziness: Warnings and Wisdom

Laziness, often referred to in scripture as sloth, is a subtle yet dangerous adversary to living a prosperous and fulfilling life. The Bible is replete with warnings against laziness and extols the virtues of diligence and hard work.

1. Understanding Laziness from a Biblical Perspective

The Bible addresses laziness directly and frequently, underscoring its significance. Proverbs 6:6-11 provides a stark warning: "Go to the ant, you sluggard; consider its ways and be wise! It has no commander, no overseer or ruler, yet it stores its provisions in summer and gathers its food at harvest. How long will you lie there, you sluggard? When will you get up from your sleep? A little sleep, a little slumber, a little folding of the hands to rest—and poverty will come on you like a thief and scarcity like an armed man."

This passage emphasizes the importance of self-motivation and foresight. The ant, without any external supervision, diligently works to prepare for the future. In contrast, laziness is depicted as a slow descent into poverty and lack. This vivid imagery serves as a powerful reminder that laziness is not merely a character flaw but a destructive force that leads to significant consequences.

2. The Detrimental Effects of Laziness

Laziness affects not only the individual but also their family, community, and society at large. Proverbs 10:4 states, "Lazy hands make for poverty, but diligent hands bring wealth." This principle is echoed throughout scripture: laziness leads to unmet needs, strained relationships, and a lack of purpose. Ecclesiastes 10:18 further warns, "Through laziness, the rafters sag; because of idle hands, the house leaks." Here, the physical consequences of neglect are highlighted, showing that laziness leads to the deterioration of what we are meant to steward.

In the New Testament, Paul addresses the issue of laziness in 2 Thessalonians 3:10-12: "For even when we were with you, we gave you this rule: 'The one who is unwilling to work shall not eat.' We hear that some among you are idle and disruptive. They are not busy; they are busybodies. Such people we command and urge in the Lord Jesus Christ to settle down and earn the food they eat." This directive from Paul reinforces the idea that productive work is essential for sustaining oneself and contributing to the community.

3. Wisdom for Cultivating a Diligent Spirit

Avoiding laziness requires intentionality and wisdom. The Bible offers several strategies to cultivate diligence and overcome slothfulness:

a. Embrace the Virtue of Hard Work:
Colossians 3:23-24 advises, "Whatever you do, work at it with all your heart, as working for the Lord, not for human masters, since you know that you will receive an inheritance from the Lord as a reward. It is the Lord Christ you are serving." This perspective transforms our view of work from a mundane task to an act of worship. When we work diligently as unto the Lord, we honor Him and reflect His character.

b. Develop a Vision and Set Goals:

Proverbs 29:18 reminds us, "Where there is no vision, the people perish." Setting goals and having a vision provides direction and motivation. It helps us stay focused and diligent, preventing the aimlessness that often accompanies laziness. Pray for God's guidance in setting goals that align with His will and purpose for your life.

c. Seek Accountability and Community:

Hebrews 10:24-25 encourages believers to "consider how we may spur one another on toward love and good deeds, not giving up meeting together, as some are in the habit of doing, but encouraging one another—and all the more as you see the Day approaching." Surrounding yourself with a community of believers who encourage and hold you accountable can be instrumental in overcoming laziness. They can provide support, encouragement, and motivation to stay diligent.

d. Cultivate Self-Discipline:

2 Timothy 1:7 declares, "For the Spirit God gave us does not make us timid, but gives us power, love and self-discipline." Self-discipline is a fruit of the Spirit that enables us to stay committed to our tasks and responsibilities, even when we do not feel like it. It involves making intentional choices and developing habits that promote productivity and diligence.

e. Rely on God's Strength:

Philippians 4:13 assures us, "I can do all this through him who gives me strength." Recognize that overcoming laziness and cultivating diligence is not solely dependent on our efforts. We must rely on God's strength and seek His help through prayer and the guidance of the Holy Spirit.

4. Practical Steps to Overcome Laziness

To put these principles into practice, consider the following steps:

- Start Your Day with Prayer and Scripture: Begin each day by seeking God's guidance and strength. Meditate on His word to renew your mind and align your actions with His will.
- Create a Daily Schedule: Plan your day with specific tasks and goals. Break them down into manageable steps and prioritize them. This helps you stay focused and avoid procrastination.
- Eliminate Distractions: Identify and remove distractions that hinder your productivity. This may involve setting boundaries with technology, creating a dedicated workspace, or establishing time blocks for focused work.
- Reward Yourself: Celebrate your accomplishments and reward yourself for completing tasks. This positive reinforcement can motivate you to stay diligent and continue working towards your goals.

By applying these biblical principles and practical steps, you can overcome laziness and cultivate a diligent spirit that honors God and leads to a prosperous and fulfilling life. Remember, God's desire for you is not to live in lack but to thrive and be a blessing to others. Embrace the wisdom of His word, work diligently, and watch as He blesses the work of your hands.

Balancing Work and Rest: God's Design

Balancing work and rest is a principle deeply rooted in the Bible, reflecting God's design for human life. Here, we will explore the biblical foundation of work and rest, the importance of balance, and practical steps to achieve this balance in a way that honors God and promotes overall well-being.

1. Biblical Foundation of Work and Rest

From the very beginning, God established a rhythm of work and rest. In Genesis 1 and 2, we see God creating the world in six days and resting on the seventh. This pattern was not because God needed rest, but to set an example for us. Exodus 20:8-11 commands, "Remember the Sabbath day, to keep it holy. Six days you shall labor and do all your work, but the seventh day is a Sabbath to the Lord your God." This command underscores the importance of rest as a divine principle.

2. The Importance of Balance

Work is a divine mandate. Colossians 3:23-24 instructs us to work heartily, as for the Lord and not for men. However, excessive work can lead to burnout, stress, and a disconnect from God's purpose. On the other hand, neglecting work leads to idleness and missed opportunities to glorify God through our efforts. Proverbs 6:6-11 warns against laziness, urging us to learn from the ant's diligence. Balancing work and rest ensures we fulfill our duties without compromising our health, relationships, or spiritual growth.

3. Jesus as the Perfect Example

Jesus Christ exemplified the perfect balance of work and rest. He engaged in tireless ministry, teaching, healing, and preaching, yet He also knew the importance of withdrawing to solitary places to pray (Luke 5:16). Jesus' rhythm of ministry and solitude teaches us that rest is not a luxury but a necessity for effective service and spiritual renewal. By following Jesus' example, we find the strength and clarity to carry out our God-given tasks.

4. Practical Steps to Achieve Balance

Achieving balance requires intentionality and discipline. Here are practical steps to help maintain this balance:

a. Prioritize Time with God: Daily devotions, prayer, and Bible study should be non-negotiable. This time refuels us spiritually and provides the strength and wisdom needed for our work.

b. Set Boundaries: Establish clear boundaries between work and personal time. Learn to say no to additional tasks that encroach on your rest time. This might involve setting specific work hours and adhering to them strictly.

c. Embrace the Sabbath: Commit to observing a day of rest each week. Use this time to rest physically, reflect spiritually, and rejuvenate emotionally. Engage in activities that bring joy and relaxation.

d. Plan and Prioritize: Effective time management is crucial. Plan your week, prioritize tasks, and delegate when possible. Proverbs 21:5 says, "The plans of the diligent lead to profit as surely as haste leads to poverty."

e. Practice Self-Care: Physical health impacts our ability to work effectively. Ensure you get adequate sleep, exercise regularly, and maintain a healthy diet. Self-care is not selfish; it's essential for sustainable productivity.

5. Trusting God with Our Work

Balancing work and rest also involves trusting God with our efforts and outcomes. Psalm 127:1-2 reminds us, "Unless the Lord builds the house, those who build it labor in vain. Unless the Lord watches over the city, the watchman stays awake in vain. It is in vain that you rise up early and go late to rest, eating the bread of anxious toil; for he gives to his beloved sleep." Recognizing that our ultimate success depends on God's blessing allows us to rest without guilt or anxiety.

Balancing work and rest is a reflection of God's perfect design. It requires us to be diligent in our work, intentional in our rest, and faithful in trusting God with the results. By integrating these principles into our lives, we not only honor God but also position ourselves for greater effectiveness and fulfillment in all we do. Let us strive to find this balance, knowing that in doing so, we are walking in the footsteps of our Creator, who modeled this rhythm from the very beginning.

Cultivating a Spirit of Excellence

The spirit of excellence is a vital attribute for every Christian who desires to reflect the glory of God through their work and daily activities. It goes beyond mere competence and aims for the highest standards, mirroring the character of God in all endeavors.

Understanding the Biblical Foundation

The concept of excellence is deeply rooted in the Scriptures. Colossians 3:23-24 (NIV) states, "Whatever you do, work at it with all your heart, as working for the Lord, not for human masters, since you know that you will receive an inheritance from the Lord as a reward. It is the Lord Christ you are serving." This passage highlights the importance of wholehearted effort and dedication in all tasks, recognizing that our ultimate service is to God, not merely to human authorities.

Furthermore, Daniel is a quintessential example of a biblical character who embodied the spirit of excellence. Daniel 6:3 (NIV) records, "Now Daniel so distinguished himself among the administrators and the satraps by his exceptional qualities that the king planned to set him over the whole kingdom." Daniel's commitment to excellence set him apart and led to significant influence and responsibility. His life demonstrates that excellence attracts divine favor and opens doors for greater impact.

Practical Application of Excellence

Cultivating a spirit of excellence involves a deliberate and disciplined approach to every aspect of life. Here are key practical steps to achieve this:

1. Commitment to Lifelong Learning: Proverbs 1:5 (NIV) advises, "Let the wise listen and add to their learning, and let the discerning get guidance." A commitment to lifelong learning ensures continuous improvement and adaptation. This includes formal education, personal study, and seeking wisdom from mentors.

2. Attention to Detail: Luke 16:10 (NIV) says, "Whoever can be trusted with very little can also be trusted with much." Paying attention to the

small details reflects a dedication to excellence. This involves meticulous planning, thoroughness in execution, and ensuring quality in even the minor aspects of our work.

3. Perseverance and Diligence: Galatians 6:9 (NIV) encourages, "Let us not become weary in doing good, for at the proper time we will reap a harvest if we do not give up." Excellence requires perseverance and a diligent work ethic. It is the consistent effort and refusal to settle for mediocrity that yield outstanding results.

4. Innovation and Creativity: As beings created in the image of a creative God, we are called to innovate and think creatively. This involves looking for new and better ways to accomplish tasks, solve problems, and enhance productivity. Romans 12:2 (NIV) urges, "Do not conform to the pattern of this world, but be transformed by the renewing of your mind." Renewed thinking leads to innovative solutions and creative excellence.

5. Integrity and Character: True excellence is undergirded by integrity and moral character. Proverbs 11:3 (NIV) asserts, "The integrity of the upright guides them, but the unfaithful are destroyed by their duplicity." Excellence is not merely about performance but also about the ethical and moral standards that guide our actions.

Transformative Power of Excellence

A spirit of excellence transforms not only individual lives but also the broader community and society. When Christians embrace and exhibit excellence, they become powerful witnesses of God's glory. This transformation manifests in various ways:

- Influence and Leadership: Individuals who pursue excellence naturally rise to positions of influence and leadership. They are sought after for their reliability, wisdom, and ability to deliver exceptional results. This opens doors for sharing the gospel and impacting lives for Christ.

- Inspiration and Motivation: A commitment to excellence inspires others to elevate their standards and strive for greater achievements. It creates a culture of high performance and encourages those around to pursue their best.

- Economic and Social Development: Excellence in work leads to higher productivity, innovation, and economic growth. It contributes to the overall well-being and progress of society, aligning with the biblical mandate to be fruitful and multiply (Genesis 1:28).

Cultivating a spirit of excellence is a profound expression of our faith and devotion to God. It requires intentionality, discipline, and a relentless pursuit of the highest standards. By embodying excellence in all we do, we reflect God's character, inspire others, and contribute to the advancement of His kingdom on earth. As we strive for excellence, let us remember that we are ultimately working for the Lord, and our efforts, when done in His name, have eternal significance.

Chapter 5

Overcoming Financial Obstacles with Faith

Trusting God in Times of Financial Crisis

Financial crises are inevitable in life. Whether due to unforeseen medical expenses, job loss, economic downturns, or other unexpected circumstances, such challenges can cause significant stress and anxiety. However, as Christians, we are called to approach these situations with unwavering faith in God's provision and promises.

Understanding God's Sovereignty

The first step in trusting God during financial crises is acknowledging His sovereignty over all aspects of our lives, including our finances. Scripture reminds us that God is in control and nothing happens outside of His will. Jeremiah 29:11 states, "For I know the plans I have for you, declares the Lord, plans for welfare and not for evil, to give you a future and a hope." This assurance that God has a plan for our lives, even in times of financial distress, is foundational to our faith.

Faith in God's Provision

The Bible is replete with stories of God providing for His people in miraculous ways. Consider the story of Elijah and the widow of Zarephath (1 Kings 17:8-16). During a severe famine, God sent Elijah to a widow who had almost nothing left. Despite her dire circumstances, she obeyed God's command to provide for Elijah, and in return, God miraculously provided for her and her household. This story illustrates that God can provide for us in ways we cannot imagine, even when resources are scarce.

Practicing Contentment

In times of financial crisis, it is essential to practice contentment and gratitude for what we have. Philippians 4:12-13 teaches, "I know how to be brought low, and I know how to abound. In any and every circumstance, I have learned the secret of facing plenty and hunger, abundance and need. I can do all things through him who strengthens me." Paul's words encourage us to rely on Christ's strength and to find contentment regardless of our financial situation.

Prayer and Supplication

Prayer is a powerful tool for overcoming financial obstacles. Philippians 4:6-7 advises, "Do not be anxious about anything, but in everything by prayer and supplication with thanksgiving let your requests be made known to God. And the peace of God, which surpasses all understanding, will guard your hearts and your minds in Christ Jesus." When faced with financial difficulties, we should turn to God in prayer, presenting our needs and trusting in His peace and provision.

Community Support and Generosity

The Christian community plays a vital role in supporting one another during times of financial hardship. Acts 2:44-45 describes the early church: "And all who believed were together and had all things in common. And they were selling their possessions and belongings and distributing the proceeds to all, as any had need." This spirit of generosity and mutual support should be a hallmark of our faith communities. When we share our resources and support each other, we reflect God's love and provision.

Testimonies of Faith and Provision

Real-life testimonies of God's provision can bolster our faith and encourage us to trust Him more deeply. Hearing stories of individuals who have experienced God's miraculous provision in their financial crises can inspire us to believe that He will do the same for us. These testimonies serve as modern-day reminders of God's faithfulness and His ability to meet our needs.

Practical Steps to Trust God

- Study God's Word: Immerse yourself in Scriptures that speak about God's provision and faithfulness. Meditate on these promises and let them strengthen your faith.
- Maintain a Grateful Heart: Keep a gratitude journal to remind yourself of God's past faithfulness. Reflecting on His goodness can help shift your focus from worry to trust.
- Seek Godly Counsel: Consult with wise and godly advisors who can provide practical financial advice and spiritual encouragement.
- Serve Others: Even in financial hardship, find ways to serve and bless others. This keeps your focus outward and can open doors for God's provision.
- Trust in God's Timing: Remember that God's timing is perfect. Be patient and trust that He is working behind the scenes, even when you cannot see immediate results.

Trusting God during times of financial crisis requires a deep-rooted faith in His sovereignty, a heart of contentment, diligent prayer, and the support of a loving community. By focusing on God's promises and His past faithfulness, we can navigate financial challenges with confidence and hope, knowing that He will provide for our every need.

Stories of Faith Overcoming Financial Hardships

From Genesis to Revelation, the Bible is replete with stories of individuals and communities who, through unwavering faith in God, overcame seemingly insurmountable financial hardships. These narratives serve not only as historical accounts but as powerful testimonies and blueprints for believers today. Let's delve into these stories to understand how faith can triumph over financial adversity.

The Widow's Oil: An Overflow of Provision

One of the most compelling stories is that of the widow and the prophet Elisha in 2 Kings 4:1-7. Faced with the threat of her sons being taken as slaves to pay off her deceased husband's debts, the widow turned to Elisha for help. He asked her, "What do you have in your house?" She replied, "Your servant has nothing there at all except a small jar of olive oil."

Elisha instructed her to borrow empty jars from her neighbors and pour oil into all of them. Miraculously, the oil did not run out until every jar was filled. She sold the oil, paid her debts, and lived off the surplus. This story underscores the principle that God can multiply even the smallest resources when we act in faith and obedience. It teaches us to trust God's provision and to recognize the potential in what we already possess, however insignificant it may seem.

The Feeding of the Five Thousand: Miracles of Multiplication

In the New Testament, the story of Jesus feeding the five thousand (Matthew 14:13-21) with five loaves of bread and two fish is a profound illustration of divine multiplication. Faced with a massive crowd and limited resources, Jesus blessed the food and broke it, distributing it through His disciples. Not only was everyone fed, but twelve baskets of leftovers were collected afterward.

This miracle teaches us that when we place our limited resources in God's hands, He can multiply them beyond our expectations. It encourages believers to approach financial difficulties with a mindset of abundance, trusting that God can turn scarcity into plenty.

Job: Restoration Beyond Measure

The story of Job, detailed in the Book of Job, is one of profound suffering and ultimate restoration. Job, a wealthy man, lost all his possessions, his children, and his health. Despite his intense suffering and the misguided advice from friends, Job maintained his faith in God. His perseverance and unwavering trust were rewarded when God restored his fortunes, giving him twice as much as he had before.

Job's story emphasizes that faith in the midst of trials is crucial. It teaches us that God is a restorer and that financial hardships, no matter how severe, are not the end of the story. God's plans for us are for prosperity and not for harm, to give us hope and a future (Jeremiah 29:11).

Ruth and Naomi: Redemption through Loyalty and Faith

The book of Ruth tells the story of two widows, Naomi and her daughter-in-law Ruth, who faced severe poverty after the deaths of their husbands. Ruth's loyalty to Naomi and her faith in the God of Israel led her to glean in the fields of Boaz, a relative of Naomi. Boaz, moved by Ruth's dedication, extended his protection and generosity, eventually marrying her. Through this union, Ruth and Naomi's fortunes were restored, and they became part of the lineage of King David and ultimately Jesus Christ.

This narrative highlights the importance of faithfulness, loyalty, and the belief that God orchestrates divine connections to provide for His people. It reassures believers that God can use others to fulfill His promises and provide in ways we might not foresee.

Personal Testimonies: Modern-Day Miracles

Even today, countless believers can attest to miraculous financial turnarounds through faith. Stories abound of individuals who, through prayer, fasting, and unwavering trust in God, have seen debts canceled, unexpected job opportunities arise, and financial needs met in extraordinary ways.

These stories from the Bible and modern testimonies serve as powerful reminders that faith in God can overcome any financial hardship. They encourage us to trust in God's provision, act in obedience, and maintain a perspective of abundance. God's promises are timeless, and His provision is boundless for those who believe.

Strategies for Financial Recovery

In the face of financial adversity, Christians are called to adopt a perspective rooted in faith, wisdom, and divine principles. The journey to financial recovery can be challenging, but with God's guidance, it becomes a path of growth, resilience, and ultimately, victory. Here, we will explore detailed strategies for financial recovery from a Christian perspective, drawing on Biblical teachings and practical steps to restore financial health.

1. Recognizing the Source of Provision:

The first step in any financial recovery plan is to acknowledge that God is the ultimate source of our provision. Philippians 4:19 states, "And my God will meet all your needs according to the riches of his glory in Christ Jesus." This verse reassures believers that God's resources are limitless and He is faithful to provide for His children. In times of financial crisis, it is crucial to reaffirm our trust in God's provision and to seek His guidance in all financial matters.

2. Prayer and Fasting:

Prayer and fasting are powerful spiritual disciplines that align our hearts with God's will and invite His intervention in our financial situations.

James 1:5 encourages us to ask God for wisdom, promising that He will give it generously. Through dedicated prayer, we seek God's direction, asking for His insight on how to manage our finances, make wise decisions, and identify opportunities for recovery. Fasting, coupled with prayer, demonstrates our earnestness and dependence on God, often leading to breakthroughs and divine revelations.

3. Financial Repentance and Reconciliation:

Financial troubles can sometimes be the result of poor decisions, mismanagement, or even sinful behavior such as greed or dishonesty. Repentance involves acknowledging these mistakes before God, seeking His forgiveness, and making a commitment to change. This may also include reconciling with anyone harmed by our financial actions. Acts 3:19 advises, "Repent, then, and turn to God, so that your sins may be wiped out, that times of refreshing may come from the Lord." Repentance opens the door to God's healing and restoration.

4. Biblical Financial Principles:

To recover financially, it is essential to align our financial practices with Biblical principles. Proverbs 21:5 says, "The plans of the diligent lead to profit as surely as haste leads to poverty." This highlights the importance of careful planning and diligent effort. Budgeting, saving, and avoiding unnecessary debt are foundational practices. Proverbs 22:7 warns, "The borrower is servant to the lender," underscoring the dangers of excessive debt. Developing a realistic budget, prioritizing expenses, and setting aside savings can create a stable financial foundation.

5. Seeking Godly Counsel:

Proverbs 15:22 teaches, "Plans fail for lack of counsel, but with many advisers they succeed." Seeking advice from financially wise and spiritually mature individuals can provide valuable insights and accountability. This counsel can come from church leaders, financial advisors who share Christian values, or mentors who have successfully navigated financial challenges. These advisors can help us develop practical strategies, avoid common pitfalls, and stay focused on our recovery goals.

6. Cultivating a Spirit of Generosity:

Even in times of financial difficulty, maintaining a spirit of generosity can unlock blessings and favor from God. Luke 6:38 promises, "Give, and it will be given to you. A good measure, pressed down, shaken together and running over, will be poured into your lap. For with the measure you use, it will be measured to you." Generosity, whether through tithing, helping those in need, or supporting ministry work, invites God's provision and reflects His character. It shifts our focus from scarcity to abundance and positions us to receive God's blessings.

7. Embracing Opportunities for Growth:

Financial recovery often requires us to step out of our comfort zones and embrace new opportunities. This could mean pursuing additional education, developing new skills, or exploring alternative income streams. Ecclesiastes 11:6 encourages diversification: "Sow your seed in the morning, and at evening let your hands not be idle, for you do not know which will succeed, whether this or that, or whether both will do equally well." By diversifying our efforts, we increase the potential for financial stability and growth.

8. Maintaining Faith and Perseverance:

Finally, financial recovery is a journey that requires steadfast faith and perseverance. Hebrews 10:36 reminds us, "You need to persevere so that when you have done the will of God, you will receive what he has promised." During this process, there may be setbacks and challenges, but maintaining a strong faith in God's promises and a determined spirit will lead to eventual victory. Regularly meditating on scriptures related to God's provision and speaking affirmations of faith can keep us encouraged and focused on the goal.

Overcoming financial obstacles with faith involves a holistic approach that integrates spiritual disciplines, practical financial principles, and a heart aligned with God's will. By recognizing God as the source of our provision, engaging in prayer and fasting, practicing repentance, seeking wise counsel, embracing generosity, and persevering in faith, we can navigate the path to financial recovery with confidence and hope. Through this journey, we not only restore our financial health but also deepen our relationship with God, experiencing His faithfulness and abundance in profound ways.

The Role of Community and Support

From a Christian perspective, overcoming financial obstacles is not a solitary endeavor. The Bible emphasizes the importance of community and mutual support in many passages, illustrating that we are meant to help and uplift one another in times of need. Here, we will explore how the Christian community can play a pivotal role in helping individuals overcome financial hardships, drawing from biblical principles, historical examples, and practical applications.

Biblical Foundation

The concept of community support is deeply rooted in the Scriptures. In the early church, believers practiced communal living, sharing their resources so that no one among them was in need. Acts 2:44-45 (NIV) states, "All the believers were together and had everything in common. They sold property and possessions to give to anyone who had need." This passage highlights the sacrificial giving and unity that characterized the early Christian community.

Similarly, Galatians 6:2 (NIV) urges believers to "Carry each other's burdens, and in this way you will fulfill the law of Christ." This command underscores the importance of bearing one another's burdens, including financial ones. The community of believers is called to act as a support system, providing aid, encouragement, and resources to those facing financial difficulties.

Historical Examples

Throughout history, the Christian church has been a beacon of hope and support for those in need. During times of economic crisis, natural disasters, and wars, the church has often stepped in to provide relief. For instance, during the Great Depression in the 1930s, many churches in the United States opened soup kitchens and offered financial assistance to struggling families. This collective effort not only met immediate needs but also strengthened the bonds within the community.

In more recent times, various Christian organizations and charities continue this legacy. Organizations like World Vision, Compassion International, and local church-based food banks and financial assistance programs demonstrate the ongoing commitment of the Christian community to support those in financial distress. These efforts are not just acts of charity but manifestations of living out the Gospel's call to love and serve one another.

Practical Applications

Understanding the role of community and support in overcoming financial obstacles requires practical steps that both individuals and churches can take. Here are several actionable strategies:

- Financial Counseling and Education: Churches can offer financial literacy programs and counseling services to help members manage their finances effectively. This can include budgeting workshops, debt management seminars, and one-on-one financial coaching. By equipping individuals with knowledge and skills, the community can help prevent financial crises and promote long-term stability.

- Benevolence Funds: Many churches maintain benevolence funds specifically designated to assist members in financial emergencies. These funds can cover essential needs such as rent, utilities, medical expenses, and groceries. Establishing and contributing to such funds ensures that resources are available when unexpected financial hardships arise.

- Job Assistance Programs: The church can also play a role in helping members find employment or improve their job prospects. This can involve job fairs, resume-writing workshops, and networking opportunities. By leveraging the collective connections and expertise within the community, churches can facilitate employment opportunities and career advancement.

- Small Groups and Support Networks: Small groups within the church can serve as intimate support networks where members can share their struggles and receive encouragement and practical help. These groups foster close relationships and accountability, creating a safety net for those facing financial challenges.

- Encouraging Generosity: Teaching and modeling generosity is crucial. When individuals in the community see others giving sacrificially, it inspires a culture of generosity. Churches can highlight stories of generosity, both from the Bible and contemporary examples, to motivate members to support one another financially.

Out of the Ordinary Initiatives

Beyond the conventional methods, churches can explore innovative approaches to community support:

- Cooperative Enterprises: Churches can sponsor or facilitate cooperative businesses where members pool resources and share profits. These enterprises can range from community gardens and food co-ops to small manufacturing businesses. This not only provides income but also strengthens community bonds.

- Crowdfunding and Peer-to-Peer Lending: Leveraging technology, churches can create platforms for crowdfunding and peer-to-peer lending within the community. These platforms can help raise funds for members in need or provide interest-free loans to those facing temporary financial setbacks.

- Time Banking: Time banking is an alternative economic system where members exchange services based on time rather than money. Churches can organize time banks where individuals offer skills and services to each other, creating a supportive network that values each person's contributions.

The role of community and support in overcoming financial obstacles is a testament to the power of unity and mutual care within the Christian faith. By drawing on biblical principles, historical precedents, and practical applications, churches can effectively support their members in times of financial hardship. The Christian community, empowered by love and guided by faith, can transform lives and provide hope, demonstrating that poverty is not an option when we stand together.

Living in God's Financial Overflow

Living in God's financial overflow is not just about having an abundance of material wealth but understanding and experiencing the fullness of God's provision in every area of our lives. This concept is deeply rooted in faith, obedience, and a profound relationship with God. It involves recognizing that our ultimate source of provision is God and living in alignment with His principles to unlock the blessings He has in store for us.

Understanding God's Abundance

The Bible is replete with promises of God's provision and abundance. In John 10:10, Jesus says, "I have come that they may have life, and that they may have it more abundantly." This abundance is not limited to spiritual well-being but extends to all aspects of life, including our finances. To live in God's financial overflow, we must first understand and believe that God desires for us to prosper.

Aligning with God's Principles

Living in financial overflow requires alignment with God's principles. This involves:

- Faithful Stewardship: God entrusts us with resources, and He expects us to manage them wisely. The Parable of the Talents (Matthew 25:14-30) illustrates the importance of faithful stewardship. Those who managed their resources well were rewarded with more, while the one who did not was reprimanded. Proper management of our finances, including budgeting, saving, and investing, is crucial to experiencing financial overflow.

- Generosity: Proverbs 11:25 says, "A generous person will prosper; whoever refreshes others will be refreshed." Generosity is a key principle in God's economy. When we give, especially to those in need and to the work of God's kingdom, we open ourselves up to receive even more. It's a divine cycle of giving and receiving, reflecting God's heart of generosity.

- Obedience to God's Word: Obeying God's commandments and instructions, particularly regarding finances, positions us to receive His blessings. Malachi 3:10 challenges believers to bring the whole tithe into the storehouse and see if God will not "open the windows of heaven and pour out for you such blessing that there will not be room enough to receive it." Obedience to tithing and other biblical financial principles invites God's supernatural provision into our lives.

Cultivating a Mindset of Abundance

Living in financial overflow also involves cultivating a mindset of abundance rather than scarcity. This means:

- Trusting God Completely: Proverbs 3:5-6 instructs us to trust in the Lord with all our hearts and not lean on our understanding. Trusting God means believing that He will provide for our needs even when circumstances seem dire. It's about having unwavering faith in God's ability to supply all our needs according to His riches in glory (Philippians 4:19).

- Speaking Life Over Finances: Our words have power. Proverbs 18:21 states, "Death and life are in the power of the tongue." Speaking positively and declaring God's promises over our finances can transform our financial situation. Instead of complaining about lack, we should speak words of faith and abundance.

- Living with Gratitude: A heart of gratitude attracts God's blessings. 1 Thessalonians 5:18 encourages us to give thanks in all circumstances. Gratitude shifts our focus from what we lack to what we have, creating an atmosphere for God's blessings to flow.

Testimonies of God's Overflow

The Bible and modern testimonies abound with stories of God's miraculous financial provision. From the widow's oil in 2 Kings 4:1-7 that kept flowing until she had no more vessels to fill, to contemporary accounts of believers who have experienced unexpected financial breakthroughs, these stories serve as reminders that God's overflow is real and accessible.

Practical Steps to Living in Financial Overflow

- Commit Your Finances to God: Regularly pray over your finances, seeking God's guidance and blessing.

- Practice Generosity: Make giving a regular part of your financial plan. Support your church, missionaries, and those in need.
- Educate Yourself Financially: Gain knowledge on managing finances effectively. Read books, attend seminars, and seek counsel from wise financial advisors.
- Stay Connected to the Source: Maintain a strong relationship with God through prayer, worship, and reading His Word. This connection keeps you aligned with His will and opens the door for His blessings.

Living in God's financial overflow is a journey of faith, obedience, and alignment with His principles. It's about recognizing God as our ultimate provider and trusting Him to meet our needs abundantly. As we faithfully steward what He has given us, practice generosity, and cultivate a mindset of abundance, we position ourselves to experience the fullness of God's financial blessings in our lives.

Chapter 6

Divine Strategies for Financial Increase

Understanding God's Strategies for Wealth

In the Christian worldview, wealth is not merely a collection of material possessions or a measure of earthly success. Instead, it is viewed as a resource entrusted by God to His people for the purpose of fulfilling His divine plan. Understanding God's strategies for wealth involves recognizing the principles laid out in Scripture and aligning one's life with God's intentions. This approach transcends the ordinary perspectives on wealth, demanding a radical, faith-driven mindset that sees beyond the temporal and into the eternal purposes of God.

1. Divine Ownership and Stewardship

The foundational principle in understanding God's strategy for wealth is recognizing His ownership of all things. Psalm 24:1 declares, "The earth is the Lord's, and everything in it, the world, and all who live in it." This acknowledgment shifts our perspective from seeing wealth as something we own to something we steward. As stewards, our role is to manage God's resources wisely, in a manner that honors Him and advances His kingdom. This stewardship involves being diligent, prudent, and accountable, knowing that one day we will give an account of how we managed His assets.

2. The Principle of Seedtime and Harvest

One of the most profound strategies God has embedded in the fabric of creation is the principle of seedtime and harvest. Galatians 6:7 states, "Do not be deceived: God cannot be mocked. A man reaps what he sows." This principle applies not only to agriculture but to every aspect of life, including finances. By sowing seeds of generosity, hard work, and faith, believers can expect a harvest of blessing. This principle calls for intentionality in giving, investing, and working, knowing that each seed sown in faith will yield a return according to God's timing and purpose.

3. Faith-Filled Vision and Planning

Proverbs 29:18 tells us, "Where there is no vision, the people perish." God's strategy for wealth includes imparting vision to His people. A vision provides direction, purpose, and motivation. However, a vision without a plan remains a mere dream. Thus, believers are encouraged to seek God's guidance in their financial planning. James 4:13-15 reminds us to submit our plans to the Lord, acknowledging His sovereignty over our future. By aligning our financial goals with God's vision, we position ourselves to receive His favor and guidance in our endeavors.

4. Wisdom and Prudence

The book of Proverbs is replete with wisdom on financial matters. Proverbs 3:13-14 says, "Blessed are those who find wisdom, those who gain understanding, for she is more profitable than silver and yields better returns than gold." Wisdom in financial matters involves making prudent decisions, avoiding debt, and seeking counsel. It requires a disciplined approach to spending, saving, and investing, ensuring that every decision is made with foresight and understanding. God's strategy for wealth is not about quick riches but about sustainable and responsible growth that honors Him.

5. Divine Favor and Open Doors

Lastly, understanding God's strategy for wealth includes recognizing the role of divine favor. Proverbs 10:22 states, "The blessing of the Lord brings wealth, without painful toil for it." While hard work and diligence are essential, they are complemented by God's favor, which can open doors that no man can shut (Revelation 3:8). This favor can manifest in various ways—unexpected opportunities, divine connections, and supernatural provision. Believers are encouraged to remain faithful and obedient, trusting that God will orchestrate circumstances to bring about His purposes and bless His people.

God's strategies for wealth are deeply rooted in principles that promote stewardship, faith, wisdom, and divine favor. By understanding and applying these principles, believers can navigate the complexities of financial matters with confidence and purpose, knowing that their wealth is ultimately for the glory of God and the advancement of His kingdom. This perspective transforms the pursuit of wealth from a self-centered endeavor to a God-centered mission, filled with eternal significance and impact.

The Role of Vision and Planning

In the journey to financial increase, vision and planning are pivotal elements. These concepts are deeply rooted in biblical teachings and the character of God Himself. God is a master planner, as evidenced in the creation narrative, the detailed instructions given for building the Ark of the Covenant, and the strategic plans laid out for Israel's conquest of Canaan. Vision and planning are not just secular business concepts; they are divine principles that Christians are called to embrace and implement.

Understanding Divine Vision

Vision is the God-given ability to see beyond the present and into the future. It is the capacity to perceive what could be, rather than what is. Proverbs 29:18 states, "Where there is no vision, the people perish." This verse underscores the critical importance of vision in the life of a believer. Without a clear vision, individuals can become aimless, drifting through life without purpose or direction.

From a Christian perspective, divine vision begins with seeking God's will for our lives. It requires prayer, fasting, and meditation on God's Word to discern His plans and purposes. Jeremiah 29:11 reassures us, "For I know the plans I have for you, declares the Lord, plans for welfare and not for evil, to give you a future and a hope." God's vision for our lives is always good, filled with hope and prosperity.

Developing a God-Centered Vision

Developing a God-centered vision involves aligning our desires and plans with God's purposes. This alignment ensures that our vision is not self-serving but seeks to glorify God and advance His kingdom. Here are key steps to develop a God-centered vision:

- Seek Divine Guidance: Start with prayer, asking God to reveal His vision for your life. James 1:5 encourages us, "If any of you lacks wisdom, let him ask of God, who gives to all liberally and without reproach, and it will be given to him." Seeking God's wisdom is the foundation of a God-centered vision.

- Write the Vision: Habakkuk 2:2 instructs, "Write the vision and make it plain on tablets, that he may run who reads it." Writing down your vision solidifies it, making it tangible and actionable. It serves as a constant reminder of God's plans and keeps you focused on the goal.

- Align with Scripture: Ensure that your vision aligns with biblical principles. God's Word is a lamp to our feet and a light to our path (Psalm 119:105). It provides the guidelines and boundaries within which our vision should operate.

- Consult Wise Counsel: Proverbs 15:22 advises, "Without counsel plans fail, but with many advisers they succeed." Seeking the counsel of godly mentors and advisors can provide additional insight and confirmation of your vision.

Strategic Planning: Implementing the Vision

Once the vision is clear, the next step is strategic planning. Planning is an act of faith, demonstrating trust in God's provision and timing. Proverbs 16:3 reminds us, "Commit your work to the Lord, and your plans will be established." Effective planning involves several key components:

- Set Specific Goals: Break down the vision into specific, measurable goals. These goals should be time-bound and realistic, providing a clear roadmap for achieving the vision.

- Create a Plan of Action: Develop a step-by-step plan outlining the actions needed to reach each goal. This plan should include resources, timelines, and potential obstacles.

- Be Diligent and Disciplined: Proverbs 21:5 says, "The plans of the diligent lead surely to abundance." Diligence and discipline are essential in executing the plan. It requires consistent effort and perseverance.

- Trust in God's Timing: Ecclesiastes 3:1 reminds us, "To everything there is a season, and a time for every matter under heaven." Trusting in God's timing is crucial. While planning, remain flexible and open to God's leading and adjustments.

- Pray Continuously: Continual prayer is vital throughout the planning and implementation process. Philippians 4:6 encourages us, "Do not be anxious about anything, but in everything by prayer and supplication with thanksgiving let your requests be made known to God." Prayer keeps us connected to God, ensuring that our plans stay aligned with His will.

Bold Steps of Faith

Bold steps of faith are often required to bring a vision to fruition. Hebrews 11:1 defines faith as "the assurance of things hoped for, the conviction of things not seen." Acting on faith means taking risks, stepping out of comfort zones, and trusting God to provide and guide each step of the way.

One powerful biblical example of vision and planning is Nehemiah's rebuilding of the walls of Jerusalem. Nehemiah had a clear vision, sought

God's guidance, and strategically planned the reconstruction. Despite opposition and challenges, his faith and diligence led to the successful completion of the project, bringing glory to God.

The role of vision and planning in financial increase from a Christian perspective is foundational. It involves seeking God's guidance, aligning with His Word, setting specific goals, and taking bold steps of faith. As believers, we are called to dream big, plan diligently, and trust in God's provision, knowing that with Him, poverty is not an option.

Biblical Investments and Savings

In the realm of financial prosperity, the principles of investment and savings hold significant importance. From a Christian perspective, these principles are deeply rooted in Scripture and can be applied to our lives to ensure not only personal financial stability but also to extend God's Kingdom on earth.

Understanding Biblical Investments

Investing, in the biblical sense, goes beyond the mere act of putting money into stocks, bonds, or other financial instruments. It encompasses the idea of sowing seeds for a future harvest. The Bible is replete with agricultural metaphors that illustrate this concept. In Ecclesiastes 11:1-2, Solomon writes, "Cast your bread upon the waters, for you will find it after many days. Give a portion to seven, or even to eight, for you know not what disaster may happen on earth." This passage encourages diversification in investments, warning against putting all resources in one basket.

Investments are seen as a form of stewardship. In the Parable of the Talents (Matthew 25:14-30), Jesus commends the servants who invest their master's money and generate a return, while the servant who hides the money out of fear is reprimanded. This parable underscores the importance of wisely using and multiplying the resources God entrusts to us.

Principles of Biblical Savings

Savings, from a biblical perspective, is the prudent allocation of resources to prepare for future needs. Proverbs 21:20 says, "The wise store up choice food and olive oil, but fools gulp theirs down." This verse highlights the wisdom in setting aside resources, contrasting it with the foolishness of consuming everything without thought for the future.

Joseph's story in Genesis 41 offers a profound example of biblical savings. When Pharaoh dreams of seven years of plenty followed by seven years of famine, Joseph advises him to store a portion of the surplus during the good years. This act of saving not only ensures Egypt's survival during the famine but also positions the nation as a provider to surrounding regions. Joseph's strategic planning and foresight illustrate the godly wisdom in preparing for lean times.

Practical Steps for Biblical Investments and Savings

- Seek Divine Guidance: Prayer is paramount when making investment decisions. James 1:5 promises, "If any of you lacks wisdom, let him ask of God, who gives to all liberally and without reproach, and it will be given to him." Seek God's wisdom to discern the best opportunities and avoid potential pitfalls.

- Diversify Wisely: As Ecclesiastes 11:2 suggests, diversification is key. Spread investments across different sectors to minimize risk. This could include stocks, real estate, mutual funds, or starting a business. The goal is to create a balanced portfolio that can weather economic fluctuations.

- Prioritize Ethical Investments: Ensure that your investments align with Christian values. Avoid companies or industries that engage in practices contrary to biblical principles, such as exploitation, environmental harm, or unethical business practices. Instead, support ventures that promote social good, fair trade, and ethical standards.

- Establish an Emergency Fund: Begin by saving a portion of your income regularly to build an emergency fund. This fund should cover three to six months of living expenses. It acts as a financial buffer against unforeseen circumstances, such as job loss or medical emergencies.

- Plan for the Long Term: Biblical savings is not just for immediate needs but also for future generations. Proverbs 13:22 says, "A good person leaves an inheritance for their children's children." Consider retirement accounts, college savings plans, and other long-term investment vehicles that ensure financial stability for your descendants.

The Spiritual Impact of Biblical Investments and Savings

Investing and saving are not merely financial activities; they are spiritual disciplines that reflect our trust in God's provision and our commitment to His Kingdom. When we manage our resources wisely, we honor God as the ultimate owner of all we possess. Moreover, by creating financial stability, we position ourselves to be generous givers, supporting ministries, missions, and those in need.

The act of saving and investing also demonstrates our faith in God's provision for the future. It acknowledges that while we trust God to meet our daily needs, we also have a responsibility to manage the blessings He provides with wisdom and foresight.

Biblical investments and savings are crucial elements of financial stewardship. They require a balanced approach, grounded in prayer, ethical considerations, and practical planning. By following these principles, believers can ensure not only their own financial stability but also contribute to the expansion of God's Kingdom on earth.

Entrepreneurship and God's Favor

Entrepreneurship, when approached from a Christian perspective, is not just about business ventures or making profits. It is about recognizing and harnessing the gifts and talents that God has bestowed upon us to create value, serve others, and glorify Him. The Bible is replete with principles and examples that can guide believers in their entrepreneurial pursuits, ensuring that their endeavors are aligned with God's will and blessed with His favor.

Understanding God's Call to Entrepreneurship

God has uniquely gifted each individual with talents, skills, and passions. As it says in Ephesians 2:10, "For we are God's handiwork, created in Christ Jesus to do good works, which God prepared in advance for us to do." This verse highlights that we are created for a purpose, and for many, this purpose may be realized through entrepreneurship. Recognizing this call is the first step towards aligning one's business with God's plan.

Biblical Foundations for Business Ventures

The Bible provides numerous examples of successful entrepreneurs who were blessed by God. Consider the story of Joseph, who rose from being a slave to becoming the second most powerful man in Egypt, effectively managing the nation's resources during a time of famine (Genesis 41). His story teaches us the importance of wisdom, integrity, and reliance on God in business.

Similarly, the Proverbs 31 woman is often highlighted as a model of industriousness and entrepreneurial spirit. She engages in profitable trading, manages her household efficiently, and her works bring her praise (Proverbs 31:10-31). This passage demonstrates that entrepreneurship is not limited to men and that women, too, can be powerful instruments in God's plan for economic provision and impact.

Aligning Business Practices with Christian Values

Christian entrepreneurs are called to uphold principles of integrity, honesty, and fairness. Colossians 3:23 advises, "Whatever you do, work at it with all your heart, as working for the Lord, not for human masters." This means that every business decision and practice should reflect our commitment to Christ. It involves treating employees, customers, and competitors with respect and fairness, ensuring that our business practices are ethical and just.

Moreover, businesses should seek to serve the community and meet needs. Jesus taught us to love our neighbors as ourselves (Matthew 22:39), and this principle should be evident in how we conduct our business. This might involve providing excellent products or services, creating job opportunities, or supporting charitable causes.

Prayer and Dependence on God

Entrepreneurs face numerous challenges and uncertainties. It is crucial to maintain a close relationship with God through prayer, seeking His guidance in every decision. Proverbs 3:5-6 encourages us to "Trust in the Lord with all your heart and lean not on your own understanding; in all your ways submit to him, and he will make your paths straight." This reliance on God ensures that our business is under His protection and direction.

Experiencing God's Favor

God's favor is essential for any business to thrive. His favor opens doors that no man can shut, provides opportunities, and grants success that human effort alone cannot achieve. Psalm 90:17 says, "May the favor of the Lord our God rest on us; establish the work of our hands for us— yes, establish the work of our hands." This prayer should be at the heart of every Christian entrepreneur's endeavors.

Experiencing God's favor also means being attuned to His voice, ready to pivot or change direction as He leads. It involves stepping out in faith, sometimes taking risks, knowing that God is in control. It means celebrating successes with humility, recognizing that every achievement is a testament to His grace.

Building a Kingdom-Impacting Business

Ultimately, Christian entrepreneurship is about more than personal success or wealth. It is about building a business that impacts the Kingdom of God. This might be through direct evangelism, supporting ministry work, or creating a business culture that reflects Christian values and attracts others to Christ. It is about using the resources and platform God has given to influence the world positively and advance His Kingdom.

Entrepreneurship and God's favor are deeply intertwined when approached with a heart fully surrendered to His will. By aligning our business practices with biblical principles, maintaining integrity, relying on God through prayer, and seeking His favor, Christian entrepreneurs can build successful, impactful businesses that glorify God and serve His purposes on earth.

Multiplying What You Have: The Miracle of Increase

The principle of multiplication is one of the most powerful and profound truths found in the Bible. From the parable of the talents to the feeding of the five thousand, the Bible is replete with examples of how God takes what is small and insignificant in the eyes of man and multiplies it beyond measure. Understanding and applying this principle can transform not only our financial situation but also our entire approach to life and faith.

The Biblical Foundation of Multiplication

In Matthew 25:14-30, Jesus shares the Parable of the Talents, a story about a master who entrusts his servants with various amounts of money before leaving on a journey. The servants who actively worked and multiplied their master's money were rewarded, while the one who did nothing out of fear was reprimanded and had his talent taken away. This parable highlights several key principles of multiplication:

- Faithfulness in Small Things: God expects us to be faithful stewards of what He has given us, no matter how small it may seem. Luke 16:10 says, "Whoever can be trusted with very little can also be trusted with much." Faithfulness in small things paves the way for greater responsibilities and blessings.

- Active Participation: The servants who multiplied their talents took initiative and actively engaged in trade. Similarly, we must be proactive in using our gifts, talents, and resources, trusting that God will bless our efforts.

- Trust and Fearlessness: The servant who buried his talent acted out of fear. Fear can paralyze us and prevent us from stepping out in faith. Trusting in God's provision and stepping out in boldness is crucial for experiencing the miracle of multiplication.

The Power of Seed Faith

The concept of seed faith, as taught by Jesus, is another foundational principle of multiplication. In Mark 4:30-32, Jesus compares the Kingdom of God to a mustard seed, which is the smallest of all seeds but grows to become the largest of all garden plants. This illustrates that even the smallest acts of faith and obedience can produce significant results.

When we give, serve, or invest our resources, we are essentially planting seeds. Galatians 6:7-9 encourages us not to grow weary in doing good, for at the proper time we will reap a harvest if we do not give up. The key is to plant with expectation, knowing that God will bring the increase.

Practical Steps to Multiplication

- Identify Your Seed: Take inventory of what you have. This could be financial resources, talents, time, or even relationships. Ask God to reveal the potential within these resources and how they can be used for His glory.

- Sow Generously: 2 Corinthians 9:6 states, "Whoever sows sparingly will also reap sparingly, and whoever sows generously will also reap generously." Generosity is a catalyst for multiplication. When we give freely, God honors our faith and multiplies our seed.

- Partner with God: Acknowledge that God is the ultimate source of multiplication. Proverbs 3:5-6 advises us to trust in the Lord with all our heart and lean not on our own understanding. Invite God into your plans and rely on His wisdom and guidance.

- Expect a Harvest: Faith is the assurance of things hoped for, the conviction of things not seen (Hebrews 11:1). Approach your efforts with expectancy, believing that God will honor His promise to multiply your seed.

Testimonies of Multiplication

Throughout history, countless individuals have experienced the miracle of multiplication through their faith and obedience. Consider the story of George Müller, a Christian evangelist and director of the Ashley Down orphanage in Bristol, England. Müller relied entirely on prayer and faith for the provision of his orphanages, never asking for financial support. Yet, through his unwavering faith, God multiplied the resources, providing abundantly for thousands of children over the years.

Another example is the modern-day testimonies of believers who have stepped out in faith to start businesses, ministries, or charitable organizations with limited resources. Through their trust in God and diligent work, they have seen exponential growth and impact.

Multiplying what you have is not just about financial gain; it's about living a life of faith and trust in God's provision. It's about recognizing that God can take the little we offer and turn it into something extraordinary. As we faithfully steward our resources, sow generously, and partner with God, we can expect to see the miraculous multiplication of our efforts, bringing glory to God and advancing His Kingdom. Embrace the principle of multiplication and watch as God transforms your life and resources in ways you never imagined.

Chapter 7

Living a Life of Generosity and Impact

The Joy of Generosity

Generosity is more than just an act of giving; it is a profound expression of God's love and a testament to our faith in His provision. In a world that often emphasizes accumulation and personal gain, the Christian perspective on generosity stands out as a radical, counter-cultural approach to living.

The Biblical Foundation of Generosity

The Bible is replete with teachings on generosity. One of the most compelling passages is found in 2 Corinthians 9:7, where Paul writes, "Each of you should give what you have decided in your heart to give, not reluctantly or under compulsion, for God loves a cheerful giver." This verse encapsulates the essence of Christian giving—it is not about the amount given but the heart behind the gift. God delights in a giver who finds joy in the act of giving.

Generosity is rooted in the character of God Himself. John 3:16 declares, "For God so loved the world that He gave His one and only Son, that whoever believes in Him shall not perish but have eternal life." God's ultimate act of generosity, giving His Son for the salvation of humanity, sets the standard for how we should give—freely, sacrificially, and joyfully.

Experiencing the Joy of Generosity

The joy of generosity is multifaceted. Firstly, it comes from knowing that our giving aligns us with God's will and character. When we give, we mirror the generous heart of our Creator, participating in His divine nature. This alignment brings a deep sense of fulfillment and purpose.

Secondly, generosity shifts our focus from ourselves to others. In Acts 20:35, Paul reminds us of Jesus' words, "It is more blessed to give than to receive." When we give, we break free from the chains of selfishness and materialism, experiencing the freedom that comes from prioritizing the needs of others over our own.

Practical Ways to Live Generously

Living a life of generosity does not always require grand gestures or substantial financial resources. It begins with a mindset and is expressed through everyday actions. Here are practical ways to cultivate and experience the joy of generosity:

1. Time and Attention: Often, the most valuable gift we can offer is our time. Volunteering at a local shelter, mentoring a young person, or simply being present for someone in need demonstrates the love of Christ in tangible ways.

2. Talents and Skills: Each of us has unique talents and skills that can bless others. Whether it's offering professional expertise pro bono, teaching a skill, or using creative talents to serve the church, our abilities can be powerful tools for generosity.

3. Financial Resources: While financial giving is a significant aspect of generosity, it is not limited to large donations. Consistently supporting your local church, contributing to mission work, or helping a neighbor in need are all impactful ways to give financially.

4. Acts of Kindness: Small acts of kindness, such as paying for someone's meal, offering a ride, or sending an encouraging note, can have a profound impact. These acts create ripples of kindness that extend far beyond the initial gesture.

The Impact of Generosity

The impact of generosity extends beyond the immediate recipient. It fosters a culture of giving within our communities and churches, inspiring others to adopt a similar mindset. Generosity also opens doors for the gospel, as our actions often speak louder than words. When people see the selfless love of Christ demonstrated through our giving, they are drawn to the source of that love.

Moreover, generosity has a transformative effect on the giver. It cultivates gratitude, reduces anxiety about material needs, and strengthens our faith as we witness God's provision in response to our giving. Proverbs 11:25 says, "A generous person will prosper; whoever refreshes others will be refreshed." This verse highlights the reciprocal nature of generosity—the more we give, the more we are blessed.

Living a life of generosity and experiencing its joy requires intentionality and a heart attuned to God's purposes. As we embrace the joy of giving, we not only fulfill God's command but also unlock a deeper, more fulfilling way of life. In doing so, we become channels of God's love and provision, impacting the world around us for His glory.

Biblical Examples of Generous Living

In the vast narrative of the Bible, we encounter numerous examples of individuals who epitomized the essence of generous living. These stories not only illustrate the transformative power of generosity but also serve as timeless lessons on how God blesses and multiplies the resources of those who give from the heart. Let us explore these inspiring accounts, drawing profound insights that can guide us in our own journey of generosity.

1. Abraham's Radical Generosity

Abraham, known as the father of faith, exhibited remarkable generosity throughout his life. One striking example is his encounter with Melchizedek, the king of Salem and priest of God Most High. After a victorious battle, Abraham did something extraordinary: he gave Melchizedek a tenth of everything he had (Genesis 14:20). This act of giving, known as the tithe, was a demonstration of Abraham's recognition of God's sovereignty and provision. It wasn't merely a religious duty but an expression of profound gratitude and faith. Abraham's willingness to part with a substantial portion of his wealth set a powerful precedent for the practice of tithing, illustrating that true generosity flows from a heart that acknowledges God's ultimate ownership of all resources.

2. The Widow's Mite: A Lesson in Sacrificial Giving

In the New Testament, Jesus highlights the story of a poor widow who gave two very small copper coins into the temple treasury (Mark 12:41-44). Despite her poverty, she gave all she had to live on, an act that Jesus commended as greater than the contributions of the rich who gave out of their abundance. This widow's offering teaches us that generosity is not measured by the size of the gift but by the heart and sacrifice behind it. Her story challenges us to trust God with our resources, even when it seems we have little to give. It reminds us that in God's economy, the value of a gift is not in its monetary worth but in the faith and love that accompany it.

3. The Early Church: A Community of Generosity

The early church, as described in the Book of Acts, provides a compelling model of communal generosity. Believers were known for selling their possessions and goods to distribute to anyone in need (Acts 2:45). This radical sharing was a tangible expression of their unity and love for one another. It wasn't enforced by law but was a voluntary act of caring for the community. Their generosity was rooted in their newfound faith in Christ and their understanding that all they possessed was a gift from God. This selfless lifestyle attracted many to the faith, showcasing the power of generosity to transform lives and communities.

4. Barnabas: The Son of Encouragement

Barnabas, whose name means "son of encouragement," was another notable example of generous living. He sold a field he owned and brought the money to the apostles to help those in need (Acts 4:36-37). Barnabas's generosity was not just in giving material possessions but also in supporting and encouraging others in their faith journey. His acts of kindness and support were instrumental in the growth and strength of the early Christian community. Barnabas's life teaches us that generosity encompasses both financial giving and the giving of our time, encouragement, and support to others.

5. Lydia: A Generous Businesswoman

Lydia, a dealer in purple cloth from the city of Thyatira, was a prominent businesswoman who opened her heart and home to the Apostle Paul and his companions (Acts 16:14-15). Her generosity extended beyond financial support; she provided hospitality and resources for the spreading of the gospel. Lydia's example illustrates that generosity is not limited to any particular socioeconomic status. Whether wealthy or poor, anyone can be generous. Her willingness to use her resources for God's work demonstrates how business and generosity can go hand in hand, impacting the world for Christ.

These biblical examples of generous living reveal that true generosity is rooted in a heart transformed by God's love. It challenges us to go beyond ordinary giving, to embrace a lifestyle where generosity becomes a natural outflow of our relationship with God. As we emulate these examples, we can experience the joy and blessings that come from living a life of generous impact, knowing that our giving not only meets immediate needs but also advances God's kingdom on earth.

Impacting Your Community Through Giving

Giving is a fundamental principle of the Christian faith, deeply rooted in the teachings of Jesus Christ and the apostles. The act of giving goes beyond mere charity; it is a reflection of God's love and a manifestation of our obedience to His commandments.

The Biblical Mandate for Generosity

The Bible is replete with verses that emphasize the importance of giving. In Luke 6:38, Jesus teaches, "Give, and it will be given to you. A good measure, pressed down, shaken together and running over, will be poured into your lap. For with the measure you use, it will be measured to you." This verse encapsulates the reciprocal nature of generosity; as we give, we receive blessings in return. However, the primary motivation for giving should not be to receive but to reflect God's character and love.

Identifying Needs in the Community

To impact your community effectively, it is essential to identify its needs. This requires a compassionate heart and an observant eye. Needs can vary from financial assistance, food and clothing, educational support, to emotional and spiritual guidance. Engage with community leaders, attend local meetings, and build relationships with neighbors to understand where help is most needed. Proverbs 19:17 states, "Whoever is kind to the poor lends to the LORD, and he will reward them for what they have done." By identifying and addressing specific needs, we serve not only our community but God Himself.

Strategic Giving: Beyond the Monetary

While financial donations are significant, impactful giving often involves more than money. Consider donating your time, skills, and resources. Volunteer at local shelters, mentor young people, or offer professional services pro bono. James 2:15-17 reminds us, "If a brother or sister is poorly clothed and lacking in daily food, and one of you says to them, 'Go in peace, be warmed and filled,' without giving them the things needed for the body, what good is that? So also faith by itself, if it does not have works, is dead." True generosity is holistic, addressing both physical and spiritual needs.

Creating Sustainable Solutions

To create lasting impact, it is crucial to develop sustainable solutions rather than temporary fixes. Support initiatives that promote self-sufficiency, such as job training programs, educational scholarships, and microfinance projects. Partner with local churches and organizations to establish community gardens, cooperatives, and support groups. Galatians 6:2 encourages us to "carry each other's burdens, and in this way, you will fulfill the law of Christ." Sustainable giving helps lift the burden permanently, enabling individuals and families to thrive independently.

Inspiring Others to Give

Generosity is contagious. By leading through example, you can inspire others in your community to give. Share your experiences and testimonies, highlighting the joy and fulfillment that comes from helping others.

Organize community events that encourage collective giving, such as charity runs, fundraising dinners, and volunteer days. Hebrews 10:24-25 urges us, "And let us consider how we may spur one another on toward love and good deeds, not giving up meeting together, as some are in the habit of doing, but encouraging one another—and all the more as you see the Day approaching." Your enthusiasm and commitment can ignite a culture of generosity, multiplying the impact exponentially.

Transformational Impact: Case Studies

Let's look at some real-life examples of transformational giving. Consider the story of George Müller, a Christian evangelist who established orphanages in England through prayer and faith without directly asking for funds. His unwavering trust in God's provision inspired many to give generously, impacting thousands of orphaned children. Another example is the work of Habitat for Humanity, which builds homes for those in need through the efforts of volunteers and donations. These homes provide stability, security, and hope for countless families, illustrating the profound difference that strategic, faith-driven giving can make.

A Legacy of Generosity

Impacting your community through giving is a powerful way to live out your faith and leave a lasting legacy. It requires intentionality, compassion, and a willingness to be led by the Holy Spirit. As Christians, we are called to be the light of the world and the salt of the earth (Matthew 5:13-16).

Through our generosity, we can reflect God's love, meet tangible needs, and inspire others to join us in making a difference. In doing so, we fulfill our God-given mandate to love our neighbors as ourselves and demonstrate the transformative power of a life lived for Christ.

Living a life of generosity is not just an option but a divine calling. It is through giving that we truly reflect the heart of God and make a lasting impact on the world around us. Let us embrace this calling with boldness, creativity, and unwavering faith, knowing that our efforts will bring glory to God and blessings to our communities.

Leaving a Legacy of Faith and Provision

Leaving a legacy of faith and provision is about more than just ensuring that your descendants are financially secure; it's about instilling values, principles, and a sense of divine purpose that transcends generations. This concept is deeply rooted in the Christian faith, where the blessings of God are intended to flow from one generation to the next, creating a perpetual cycle of spiritual and material prosperity.

The Biblical Foundation

The Bible is replete with examples of individuals who left behind legacies of faith and provision. One of the most prominent examples is Abraham, who is often referred to as the father of faith. God's covenant with

Abraham was not just for him but for his descendants as well. In Genesis 17:7, God says, "I will establish my covenant as an everlasting covenant between me and you and your descendants after you for the generations to come, to be your God and the God of your descendants after you." This promise encompassed not only spiritual blessings but also material wealth and prosperity.

Teaching and Modeling Faith

Leaving a legacy of faith begins with teaching and modeling faith in your daily life. Proverbs 22:6 advises, "Train up a child in the way he should go, and when he is old he will not depart from it." Parents and guardians have a crucial role in demonstrating a life of faith through their actions, decisions, and responses to life's challenges. It's about showing that trust in God is unwavering, regardless of circumstances. This includes regular prayer, involvement in church activities, and an evident reliance on God's guidance in all aspects of life.

Generosity as a Family Value

Generosity is a hallmark of the Christian faith. Teaching children and grandchildren the importance of giving is essential. Acts 20:35 reminds us, "It is more blessed to give than to receive." Families can practice this by involving their children in charitable activities, such as volunteering, donating to the needy, or supporting mission work. By doing so, children learn that their resources, whether time, talent, or treasure, are not solely for personal consumption but are also meant to bless others.

Financial Wisdom and Stewardship

Financial literacy is another critical component of leaving a legacy of provision. The Bible speaks extensively about the importance of wise stewardship. Proverbs 13:22 says, "A good person leaves an inheritance for their children's children." This verse underscores the importance of managing resources wisely to ensure that future generations can benefit. Parents should educate their children about budgeting, saving, investing, and the dangers of debt. Practical steps might include setting up savings accounts for children, teaching them about tithing, and involving them in family financial planning discussions.

Establishing a Legacy Fund

One practical way to ensure a legacy of provision is to establish a legacy fund. This could be in the form of a trust, an endowment, or other financial instruments designed to provide ongoing support for future generations. The purpose of a legacy fund is to create a lasting impact that aligns with the family's values and faith principles. For instance, a family might set up a scholarship fund to support Christian education or donate regularly to church-building projects and mission work.

Spiritual Inheritance

While material inheritance is significant, a spiritual inheritance is even more critical. Passing down a legacy of spiritual wisdom, experiences of God's faithfulness, and a strong sense of identity in Christ is invaluable. This might include documenting testimonies of God's provision and miracles in a family journal, encouraging regular family Bible study, and maintaining an open dialogue about faith and God's work in the family's life. Ephesians 1:18 emphasizes this by saying, "I pray that the eyes of your heart may be enlightened in order that you may know the hope to which he has called you, the riches of his glorious inheritance in his holy people."

Living as a Testament to God's Faithfulness

Ultimately, leaving a legacy of faith and provision means living a life that testifies to God's faithfulness and blessings. It's about being a living example of what it means to trust in God, to live generously, and to manage resources wisely. This kind of legacy not only blesses your descendants but also serves as a powerful witness to others, inspiring them to seek the same blessings and promises from God.

Leaving a legacy of faith and provision is a multifaceted endeavor that requires intentionality, wisdom, and a deep commitment to God's principles. It's about ensuring that your descendants are not only financially secure but are also grounded in their faith and equipped to continue the cycle of blessing and generosity that God has intended for His people.

Teaching the Next Generation about God's Abundance

In today's fast-paced and often materialistic world, imparting a Biblical perspective on finances to the next generation is of paramount importance. As Christians, it is our duty to equip our children and youth with the knowledge and wisdom that will enable them to live abundantly, according to God's promises. Teaching the next generation about God's abundance involves more than just financial education; it's about instilling a mindset rooted in faith, stewardship, generosity, and trust in God's provision.

Understanding God's Promises of Abundance

The Bible is replete with promises of God's provision and abundance. One of the foundational scriptures is Philippians 4:19, "And my God will supply every need of yours according to his riches in glory in Christ Jesus." This promise is not only about meeting our immediate needs but also about understanding that God's resources are limitless. Teaching children to rely on this promise can help them build a secure foundation of trust in God's provision, regardless of their financial circumstances.

Cultivating a Spirit of Gratitude and Contentment

One of the keys to understanding God's abundance is cultivating a spirit of gratitude and contentment. Hebrews 13:5 advises, "Keep your lives free from the love of money and be content with what you have, because God has said, 'Never will I leave you; never will I forsake you.'" Teaching the next generation to appreciate what they have, rather than constantly striving for more, is crucial. This involves practical steps like encouraging them to keep gratitude journals, reflect on their blessings, and express thanks regularly in prayer.

Principles of Stewardship and Responsibility

Proverbs 22:6 states, "Train up a child in the way he should go; even when he is old he will not depart from it." Teaching children about stewardship is essential in helping them manage God's resources wisely. This includes lessons on budgeting, saving, and responsible spending. Parents and mentors can create opportunities for children to practice these principles, such as giving them a small allowance and guiding them on how to allocate it for saving, spending, and giving.

Generosity: A Heart for Giving

Acts 20:35 reminds us, "It is more blessed to give than to receive." Instilling a heart of generosity in children helps them understand the joy and blessings that come from giving. This can be done through family activities that involve giving, such as participating in community service projects, donating to those in need, or supporting church missions.

Encouraging children to give from their own resources, no matter how small, fosters a habit of generosity that will last a lifetime.

Faith in Action: Practical Exercises

Faith without works is dead, as stated in James 2:17. Therefore, it's important to teach children to put their faith into action. This can be done through practical exercises such as setting financial goals for giving, creating vision boards that reflect their God-given dreams, and regularly involving them in financial decision-making processes within the family. These activities help children see the tangible impact of their faith and generosity.

Stories and Testimonies

Sharing stories and testimonies of God's provision and abundance can be a powerful way to teach the next generation. Whether it's personal stories from family members or testimonies from church, these narratives can inspire and build faith. They serve as living proof of God's faithfulness and encourage children to trust in His promises.

Biblical Literacy and Financial Wisdom

It is also essential to ensure that children are biblically literate, understanding not only the promises of God's provision but also the principles that govern His blessings. This includes studying scriptures related to wealth, generosity, and stewardship, such as the parable of the talents (Matthew 25:14-30) and the widow's offering (Mark 12:41-44). Regular Bible study and discussions about these passages can help children develop a comprehensive understanding of God's financial principles.

Encouraging a Lifelong Journey

Teaching the next generation about God's abundance is not a one-time event but a lifelong journey. It involves continuous learning, practice, and reinforcement of biblical principles. Parents and mentors should commit to ongoing discussions, regular prayer, and shared experiences that reinforce these values. By doing so, they can help the next generation build a strong, faith-based foundation for financial prosperity and a life of generous impact.

Equipping the next generation with a Christian perspective on abundance is an investment in their spiritual and financial future. By teaching them to understand and rely on God's promises, cultivate gratitude, practice stewardship, embrace generosity, and live out their faith, we prepare them to thrive in every aspect of life. This holistic approach ensures they are not only financially savvy but also spiritually grounded, ready to impact the world for God's glory.

Appreciation

Thank you for purchasing and reading my book. I am extremely grateful and hope you found value in reading it. Please consider sharing it with friends and family and leaving a review online.

Your feedback and support are always appreciated and allow me to continue doing what I love.

Please go to www.amazon.com
if you'd like to leave a review.

TIMOTHY ATUNNISE's BESTSELLERS

Deliverance & Spiritual Warfare
- Monitoring spirits exposed and defeated.
- Jezebel spirit exposed and defeated.
- Marine spirits exposed and defeated.
- Serpentine spirit exposed and defeated.
- The United Kingdom of darkness exposed & defeated.
- Ahithophel Spirit Unmasked
- Kundalini Spirit Unmasked
- Prophetic warfare: Unleashing supernatural power in warfare.
- The time is now: A guide to overcoming marital delay.
- Earth moving prayers: Pray until miracles happen.
- I must win this battle: Expanded edition.
- I must my financial battle
- Essential prayers
- Open heavens: Unlocking divine blessings and breakthroughs.
- This battle ends now.
- Breaking the unbreakable
- Reversing evil handwriting
- I must win this battle - French edition.
- I must win this battle - Spanish edition.
- Ammunition for spiritual warfare
- Reversing the Irreversible
- Let there be a change.

- Total Deliverance: Volume 1
- 21 days prayer for total breakthroughs
- Warrior Mom: Defending your children in the court of heaven.
- The Power of Fathers' prayer
- Overcoming afflictions in the workplace
- The art of spiritual vision casting
- Thriving beyond letdowns: Overcoming constant disappointments
- The Anointed Intercessor: A Prayer Warrior's Calling
- Prayers of the Midnight Warriors
- Spiritual Mapping 101: A Beginner's Guide
- Deliverance from Satanic Dreams and Nightmares
- Inherited battles, victorious lives: Power to conquer ancestral strongholds and liberate your family's destiny.
- From bondage to breakthrough
- Learn to choose your battles.
- Total deliverance from spirit spouse
- Last minute miracles
- Unshackled
- Overcoming spiritual bullying & intimidation
- The heavenly advocate's handbook
- Breaking ungodly soul-ties
- It is finished
- Overcoming demonic instruments of derailment
- Pursue, overtake, and recover
- Power of midnight praise – Book 1
- Power of midnight praise – Book 2

- Defeating witchcraft attacks
- Dangerous enemies, dangerous prayers
- Rising from the dungeon of darkness

Deliverance from Witchcraft Attacks

- Deliverance from Enchantment & Black Magic
- Rise above the curse: An empowering guide to overcome witchcraft attacks.
- Breaking the Family Curse: Unraveling the Past for a Brighter Future and Transform Your Family Legacy
- Breaking Chains of Rejection: A personal deliverance manual

Weapons of Warfare

- The Name of Jesus: The unstoppable weapon of warfare
- Praise and Worship: Potent weapons of warfare
- Blood of Jesus: The ultimate weapon
- The Word of God as a weapon: A double-edged sword to bring transformation and unparallel victory in spiritual warfare.
- Praying with Power: The warrior's guide to weapon of dynamic warfare prayer
- The weapon of prophetic dreams
- Praying in tongues of heaven
- Waging war through fasting: The incontestable weapon of spiritual warfare
- The fire of God's presence: A weapon of unparallel strength & potency

- The Word of Testimony – A stealth weapon of spiritual warfare
- Angelic assistance in spiritual warfare
- The art of spiritual discernment: Your warfare advantage

Prayer Ministry
- Intercessory prayer
- Corporate prayer
- Prevailing prayer
- Imprecatory prayer
- Healing through prayer & fasting
- The prayer leader's handbook
- How to build a successful global prayer network
- Overcoming Spiritual Dryness
- Hearing & recognizing the voice of God

Power of Anointing
- The power of anointing for success: Partnering with God in extraordinary moments for great success
- The Power of Anointing for Generational Wealth
- Anointing for Disconnection

Holy Spirit
- Holy Spirit my prayer partner

14 Days Prayer & Fasting Series
- 14 Days prayer to break evil patterns.

- 14 days prayer against delay and stagnation
- 14 days prayer for a new beginning
- 14 days prayer for deliverance from demonic attacks
- 14 days prayer for total healing
- 14 days prayer for deliverance from rejection and hatred
- 14 days prayer for healing the foundations
- 14 days prayer for breaking curses and evil covenants
- 14 days prayer for uncommon miracles
- 14 days prayer for restoration and total recovery
- 14 days prayer: It's time for a change
- 14 days prayer for deliverance from witchcraft attacks
- 14 days prayer for accelerated promotion
- 14 days prayer for deliverance from generational problems
- 14 days prayer for supernatural supply
- 14 days prayer to God's will for your life
- 14 days prayer for Mountaintop Experience
- 14 days prayer for home, family and marriage restoration
- 14 days prayer to overcome stubborn situations.
- 14 days prayer for restoration of stolen destiny
- 14 days prayer for financial breakthroughs
- 14 Days Prayer for Extraordinary Success & Great Achievements
- 14 Days prayer against failure at the edge of success
- 14 Days prayer for breaking the curse of almost

7 Days Prayer & Fasting Series
- Breaking the chains of delay & waiting

- My story must change.

Personal Finances
- The art of utility bills negotiation
- From strapped to successful: Unlocking financial freedom beyond Paycheck to paycheck
- Escape the rat race: How to retire in five years or less.
- Mastering mean reversion: A guide to profitable trading, so simple a 10-year-old can understand
- Breaking the chains of debt
- Poverty is not an option

Bible Study
- The King is coming
- Seven judgments of the Bible
- The miracle of Jesus Christ
- The book of Exodus
- Lost and found: The house of Israel
- The parables of Jesus Christ
- Erased by the Cross

Fiction
- The merchant's legacy: A tale of faith and family
- A world unraptured: Brink of oblivion
- Gone: A chronicle of chaos

Family Counseling
- Healing whispers: Biblical comfort and healing for men after miscarriage

Leadership/Business
- The most intelligent woman: A woman's guide to outsmarting any room at any level
- Thriving in the unknown: Preparing children for careers that don't exist yet.
- Communication breakthrough: Cultivating deep connections through active listening.
- Overcoming Procrastination
- Raising Christian Leaders: A Parent's Guide

Spiritual Growth
- Divine Intimacy: Embracing the Transformative Power of Intimate Communion to Discover Profound Connection and Fulfillment
- 7 Steps to Receiving a Miracle
- 7 Simple Secrets to Consistent Answered Prayers
- The art of forgiving the unforgettable
- Grace Unleashed

Prophetic Books
- Walking in prophetic anointing
- Walking in prophetic authority
- Embracing the prophetic call

Personal Growth
- Divine masterpiece
- God has your back

Theology/Ministry
- Laughing Pulpit: Using humor to enhance preaching.
- Prophecies and Visions
- Understanding the Pentateuch
- Typology
- The Seven Dispensations

Parenting/Relationship
- Embracing metamorphosis: Nurturing teenage girls' remarkable journey into adulthood

Mental Health
- The power of inner healing

Marriage/Family
- The conscious husband: Mastering active listening in marriage.
- The conscious wife: Nurturing relationship with awareness, building a perfect and flourishing family.
- Conscious parenting: Mastering active listening to your children.
- From cradle to consciousness: Guiding your child's awareness

- The 'Not Tonight' syndrome: Overcoming false excuses in marital intimacy.
- 12 Practical steps to making your marriage heaven on earth
- Couple's workshop
- Sacred Intimacy

End-Times
- Dawn of eternity: Unraveling the rapture of the saints
- Signs of the end-times: Deciphering prophecies in a race against time
- The rise of the Antichrist: Unveiling the beast and the prophecies
- The Departure

Short eBooks
- Unleash the fury.
- Walking on water
- Unlonely

www.ingramcontent.com/pod-product-compliance
Lightning Source LLC
Chambersburg PA
CBHW031416210526
45464CB00005B/1914